THE GEEK SQUAD GUIDE TO SOLVING ANY COMPUTER GLITCH

The Technophobe's Guide to
Troubleshooting, Equipment,
Installation, Maintenance,

and Saving Your Data
in Almost Any Personal
Computing Crisis

ROBERT STEPHENS
with **DALE BURG**

Illustrated by Steve Mark • Poetry by Martha Rose Reeves

A FIRESIDE BOOK Published by Simon & Schuster

FIRESIDE
Rockefeller Center
1230 Avenue of the Americas
New York, NY 10020

Designed by Bonni Leon-Berman
Manufactured in the United States of America

10 9 8 7 6 5 4 3 2 1

Library of Congress Cataloging-in-Publication Data
Stephens, Robert (Robert C.), date.
The Geek Squad guide to solving any computer glitch: the technophobe's guide to troubleshoot-
    ing, equipment, installation, maintenance, and saving your data in almost any personal com-
    puting crisis / Robert Stephens with Dale Burg; illustrated by Steve Mark; poetry by Martha
    Rose Reeves.
p.   cm.
1. Microcomputers—Maintenance and repair.   2. Computer input-output equipment.   I. Burg,
    Dale.   II. Title.
TK7887.S72   1999
621.39'16—dc21   99-27116   CIP
ISBN 0-684-84343-9

ACKNOWLEDGMENTS

A very, very special debt of gratitude to my colleagues at the Geek Squad—Special Agents Ryan Austin, Andy Bork, Will Chantland, John Dahlquist, Chad Grimsrud, Steve Halligan, Tony Hartwig, Dan Jensen, Julie Kearns, Kyle Killion, Eric Kimmel, Derek Krueger, Brian Martinson, Marty Miller, Karen Ross, Peter Ryan, Robert Serr, Ryan Smith, and Matt Super. They reviewed and re-reviewed this material many times, and their contributions are evident on every page.

A thousand thanks to Terry McIntire, whose firm hand keeps us Geeks on track and without whose tenacity this book would never have been completed.

Some very gracious and encouraging publishing professionals brought this book along the road, including agent Jonathon Lazear and his associate Christie Cardenas, who helped keep the pieces in place. Thanks also to our supportive editor Tricia Medved and to Anne Bartholomew and the other members of the support staff at Simon & Schuster. Special ackowledgment to editor Sarah Baker, whose wit and humor helped give us direction at a critical juncture.

The text is greatly enhanced by the quirky poetry of Martha Rose Reeves, a poet with a law degree who lives in Boston with her LCII and her Performa 640CD. She was awarded the Jack Kerouac Literary Prize by the Lowell Celebrates Kerouac! Festival.

My gratitude to our illustrator, Steve Mark, for bringing extra humor and attitude to the pages.

Many thanks to our writer, Dale Burg, for putting up with a bunch of Geeks working on their first book and for helping save the day.

I am indebted to Dean Bachelor and all at the Platinum Group for their wisdom and support.

Special thanks to my parents, who bought me my first computer, and a very special personal acknowledgment to my wife, Shelly, who still thinks I'm a Geek.

Surely you have noticed that your computer tends to crash when you're

working on something vitally important, not when you're playing solitaire.

We think that this is definitely strange. Not that we're exactly conspiracy

theorists, but my colleagues and I at the Geek Squad in Minneapolis sometimes

think of ourselves as the technological Men in Black, dedicated to keeping the

universe as we know it free of computer breakdowns. For ten years we have

been solving problems encountered by users of every kind of computer. This

book is a compilation of everything that we've learned.

And just on the remote chance that there *is* some kind of a conspiracy, this

book is dedicated to its defeat.

CONTENTS

CONTENTS
10

CONTENTS
12

INTRODUCTION

This is a manual for people who hate to read manuals. At that horrible moment when you flip the switch or press a key and your trusty computer companion ignores your command—or rolls over and plays dead—this book should help you get it up and, if not quite running, at least limping toward help—without making you resort to a manual.

The Geek Squad defines a "computer problem" as any situation in which the computer doesn't respond to your command. Rude suggestions shouted at the machine don't count—we mean reasonable requests sent via mouse and keyboard that direct the computer to start up, modify what's on the screen, print a document, and so on. When these things don't happen on demand, people assume that the computer is "broken."

In fact, there are three possible causes for a computer problem:

- There may be something wrong with the hardware, in which case the machine or one of its devices *is* broken.
- Something is wrong with a piece of software, so a part of the operating system or one of the applications needs to be modified, replaced, or updated.
- You're the problem. We are certain that once we've explained what you're doing and you take a little personal inventory, you'll accept this diagnosis in the right spirit.

In any case, we can help.

Following a computer emergency, the first question the Geek Squad usually hears is not "How is my computer?" but "Is my data safe?" Thus, data safety is the priority in this book. Fortunately, rescuing data is often possible, and we'll tell you how to do it. We'll also help you solve many problems easily, at no cost, without any tools, and with a minimum of insanity so that you can get right back to work. And even in cases where you'll need professional help, we'll help you get it cheaper and faster, because you'll learn here how to describe and even diagnose a problem relatively accurately.

To most people, a computer is the most mysterious of all the machines that they use with any frequency. One reason is that its working parts are hidden from

view; another is that the computer acts a little like a surly Gen X movie star: it is usually so quiet that it can barely be heard (to hear the fan rotate and the hard drive spin, you have to listen very closely), but is subject to sudden and unpredictable bursts of bad behavior.

The fact is, the computer, despite its solid, stable appearance, is actually a highly sensitive creature. It works like a string of Christmas tree bulbs—if one bulb is out, the whole string goes dark. A specific problem with the hard drive, battery, screen, keyboard, or mouse can make the entire machine behave oddly or start a chain reaction that will make it balk and refuse to budge.

Computers are getting faster, better, and cheaper, but each new model comes with its own set of bugs and glitches and needs breaking in. In addition, with each new development, compatibility problems are an issue. Once upon a time, most of the hardware and software was manufactured by the same company. Not any more—when you want to perform an operation like connecting to the Internet, for instance, you're using several pieces of equipment, each likely from a different manufacturer. The central processing unit (CPU), the brain of the computer, is probably made by Intel or Motorola. The logic board, or motherboard, on which you will find the CPU chip that dispatches its commands to the various devices, is most likely produced by a subcontractor in Taiwan. And different brand names may emblazon the memory, the modem, the modem software, the Internet browser, and so on. All of them must work in well-oiled harmony.

As a result, your tech support will be unsatisfactory. The people who answer the phones follow the guidelines set out in their manuals. But if you're using a computer made by one company, a modem made by another, and a hard drive made by a third, when you call the modem people for help, they may refer you to the hard-drive specialists. And when you call them, they may send you to the computer team. You can get the sense that you're in the movie *Groundhog Day*, doomed to repeat the same conversation over and over without any progress. As if you weren't on enough of a downer, being without your trusty machine.

Problems with a computer are so devastating because the machines are so useful that we become very dependent on them. Imagine how an office worker of twenty years ago would feel if the typewriter broke, the files went up in flames, the copier exploded, the Rolodex and appointment book disappeared, and the personal assistant quit—all in the same instant. That's what it's like when a single computer goes down.

Computers will never be perfect, because they're designed and built by people, not by other computers. At the same time, however, a computer problem can always be solved—though the solution may not always be exactly what you would like it to be.

Over the past five years, the Geek Squad has solved computer problems—thousands of them—twelve hours a day, seven days a week. Once we started keeping track, it became obvious that we weren't getting calls about hundreds of different problems, but hundreds of calls about the same problems. We thought that it would be great to collect them in a book, because they are so easily solved.

We could have published this information on a CD-ROM or on the Internet, but if your computer has gone down, you can't use your CD-ROM drive or access the Internet. So, a book was the logical choice. Books have other advantages, too: they aren't very expensive, they require no batteries, they fit in your laptop bag, they boot up instantly, and they never crash. On the other hand, they can't update themselves. That's why we maintain our Web site. If you need more information, or updates on information, go to www.geeksquad.com.

Will *The Geek Squad Guide to Solving Any Computer Glitch* help you fix every problem? No. But it will help save your data, and it will help you figure out why you're having the problem and what to do about it. Plus, it will do all this in language that you can understand. To many people, tech talk sounds like Urdu. (To speakers of Urdu, we hear, techies appear to be talking in English.) The only possible explanation for computer terminology is that much of it is developed by people with no social life, which makes for a devastating combination: not only do they have plenty of free time to come up with totally incomprehensible stuff, but there is nobody around to say, "Whoa, dude, I don't know what you're talking about."

Fortunately, many computer problems are quite easy to deal with. If in a few cases we've suggested solutions that may be beyond your skills or patience level, we recommend that you go for professional help. But even if that happens, we hope to have given you something important nonetheless: a possible explanation for why the problem is there.

In any event, you're way ahead of the average person who shows up at a repair center. Most of our customers, for example, never thought of writing down the error message that their computer reported when it crashed, and can't recall whether the machine had been behaving oddly right before the crash happened. Many customers, too, give the kind of eyewitness report that would lend suspense

to many a courtroom drama, being inaccurate, useless, and/or completely wrong.

Imagine that you could go to your doctor with a medical problem and say, "Doc, I've ruled out high blood pressure, and you don't have to bother with the blood tests—I already know I've got a high sedimentation rate, and even though my cholesterol is high, so are my HDLs." You'd save time, you'd save money, and you might startle the doctor into paying extra attention to you.

Similarly, if you can tell a computer technician what kind of problem you think you have and even, following our advice, bring along a part that may need replacing, you may increase your likelihood of positive results. If the problem is relatively simple, the repairman may deal with it on the spot, and, if you have an idea of what you're talking about, you are less likely to get ripped off. You have probably seen the expression "caveat emptor." It does not mean "The cave is unoccupied." It means "Let the buyer beware." We hate to say it, but being technically clever is not necessarily related to being scrupulously honest.

We couldn't imagine writing a book about fixing computers without passing along some of the other information we've acquired over the years, such as some tips on how to buy computers and, especially, ways to prevent problems from happening. That's all in here, too. But our biggest concern is helping you solve problems that have already occurred. This book is organized along a timeline, starting with the problems you might encounter from the moment you turn the computer on (or *try* to) and continuing step by step as your screen appears, your hard drive boots up, and so on.

Most of the advice in here will apply to any kind of computer. That's because there are only three computer operating systems in widespread use—Windows 3.X (DOS), Windows95 and its baby brother 98 (which we've treated as the same, since in terms of troubleshooting, they pretty much are), and Mac. DOS is becoming obsolete and Windows is becoming more and more like Mac. In the few cases where different solutions are needed, you'll find them.

Some people have asked us if we're concerned that giving away our secrets will put us out of business. No way—as long as there are millions of VCRs across America blinking "12:00," we've got a customer base, and we're there for them. Be grateful to the people who own those VCRs. They have funded all the research that has resulted in the advice you're about to receive.

If you can't have a Geek Squad member at your side when something goes wrong, *The Geek Squad Guide to Solving Any Computer Glitch* is the next best thing.

USING THIS BOOK

Throughout *The Geek Squad Guide to Solving Any Computer Glitch,* we employ a few pieces of shorthand. A key:

 Geek Technique. An extra little suggestion or tip; or what to tell the pro when you bring the computer in for repair.

Caution. Take extra care in performing the suggested task.

| = "Next click on [whatever follows]." It seemed preferable to saying, "First click on this, and then click on that, and then click on a third item," over and over again.

+ = When keys should be held down at the same time, we use a plus sign to connect them. For example, "Shift+A" directs you to hit the A key while holding down Shift.

Whenever you see numbers, it means to try the steps *in order.*

Chapter One

CHOOSING A COMPUTER

To PC or not to PC: A Windows-based machine or a Mac? Laptop or desktop? A new computer or a used one? What to buy depends on your needs. If you're just using your computer to write letters and do your income tax, you need only the simplest setup. If you're planning to get involved in desktop publishing, you need lots of memory to handle the graphics. A desktop computer is fine if you plan to use it in one place, but you should consider a laptop if you're bringing it along to the library, to meetings, to Club Med. (To Club Med? Are you sure?) We can help you weigh the options, but the ultimate decision is very much a personal one.

Comparing Brands: Windows-Based Computers vs. Macintosh

The first big decision is which operating system to choose. We have always had a special thing about Macintosh computers—when the Geek Squad started out, we ran our whole business with them. Though you may have heard about problems with Apple machines in the past, the new ones are very, very good.

You also need never worry about Apple going out of business. Naturally, you don't want to be left stranded on the Planet of the Windows-Based Computers with the last Mac in existence, at a loss for service or equipment. But that is a scenario that will not take place. A couple of years ago, there were about 20 million Mac users around the world—of every hundred personal computers, five were Macs—and the number hasn't dropped appreciably. As long as there are some 20 million customers relying on these machines, there will be spare parts manufactured and servicepeople who will figure out how to take care of them. If you love your Mac, if you don't care to learn a new system, if you're already heavily invested in Mac, there's no reason not to stick with it.

On the other hand, if you're open to change or you're making your first purchase, we'd point you toward one of the Windows-based computers.

Here are some of the pros and cons of both Windows-based systems and Macs.

Features: Windows took some of the great Mac innovations and improved on them. So now Windows machines offer most of them, and more. However, with respect to desktop publishing or working with graphics, Macs have the edge—they just make it easier.

Performance: While some of the new Macs have faster processors, that's only one measure of performance. Windows 95/98 seems to some of us to be faster and more efficient when running several applications at once—for example, when you're working on a couple of graphics programs and a word-processing program simultaneously. Even the Internet seems to run faster in a Windows environment than on a Mac.

Price: Windows-based computers cost less than Macs because several companies make them, and only Apple makes Macs. And because several companies make Windows-based computers, replacement parts for them are easier to get.

Reliability: Machines using Windows crash less often than Macs. That's because Windows uses a system called "preemptive multitasking," while Macs use "cooperative multitasking." What that means in English is that in a crash, Windows limits any damage to the programs that you were working on at the time of the crash, whereas a Mac can create random havoc throughout the system. On the other hand, hardware and software incompatibility, the cause of all sorts of problems, will always be an issue with Windows because Microsoft makes the operating system and other companies make the hardware. With Mac, it's one company ships all—Apple makes both the operating system and the hardware.

Ease of operation: In a study of users who worked with both types of machines, two-thirds said that Macs were easier to troubleshoot, three-quarters said that it was easier to connect peripheral devices to a Mac, and nearly that many said that Macs were generally easier to set up and install. In another study, people who used both machines said that Mac maintenance required less time, less knowledge of computers, and less tech support.

Availability of software: Although major programs are available for both operating systems, and you can probably get anything you need for a Mac format, it's largely a Windows world. Many of the newest programs are being made for Windows only.

Compatibility: If you want to have the least amount of trouble exchanging disks and information, you're better off with Macs. Macs can read disks from PCs, but PCs cannot automatically read from a Mac.

SUMMARY		
CRITERIA	MAC	WINDOWS
Word processing, spreadsheets, databases		Winner
Desktop publishing, creating graphics, drawing	Winner	
Performance	Tie	Tie
Price		Winner (generally)
Reliability		Winner
Setup and installation	Winner	
Maintenance	Winner	
Adding peripherals, transferring applications, programs, drives, and modems	Winner	
Troubleshooting	Winner	
Availability of software		Winner
Exchanging information	Winner	

Bottom line: All things considered, and even if Macs lead in more categories, we believe that Windows has the edge. But anyone who is heavily invested in Macs should stick with them, and so should anyone who just happens to prefer them. Being able to say "I like it better" is the most valid reason for choosing a particular system. Because, hey, you're the one who's living with it.

Buying a Used Computer

In general, we recommend against buying a used computer. The price differential between new and used isn't that great, and with a new one, you get all the bells and whistles, and the machine is covered by a warranty.

Two exceptions: A used computer is fine as a backup machine and as a machine for the kids to play games on. (Under no circumstances consider sharing a computer with any child who is not old enough to vote: when Junior plays the latest shoot-'em-up intergalactic laser-blaster game he's downloaded from the Internet and blasts the bad guys into oblivion, he may send your financial files along with them.)

If you do consider buying a used computer, remember that it is not like buying a used car. There are only two moving parts to a computer—the fan and the hard drive—and they need only occasional maintenance and servicing, so wear and tear is not the issue. A FOR SALE sign on a computer is not usually code for "I'm trying to unload this clunker," but an indication that the owner has probably used it for two or three years and is now ready for something more sophisticated and faster. What's obsolete for somebody else may be just fine for you.

One dog year equals seven human years. One computer year is like twenty-five human years. The lesson here is, don't buy a used machine that is more than three years old. Most hard drives and power supplies begin to fail after three to four years.

Companies that are updating their computer equipment are a great source of used machines. So are used computer stores, and unlike an individual (and probably unlike a company), a store will probably give you a warranty, though it may cover you for only one year, or three at most. If you have the chance to take or continue an existing service plan, do it. For a $500 computer, extending the plan might set you back $50 to $70 per year. That's a bargain when you consider that a repair shop would charge you between

$100 and $200 an hour—more if the technician has to make a house call.

There's not much you can check out when buying a used machine, but there are at least a couple of questions you should ask: First, can it take you to the Internet? Just about all of the newer machines can. And second, does it come with a warranty? Most warranties are transferable.

Often, computer manufacturers will preinstall software, including the operating system. When you buy the machine, ownership of the software is included. Get backup copies of the original installation disks or CD, because when the machine has a problem, reinstalling the system is often an easy cure. If you don't have the system software, you can't do that. A retailer who can't give you the software at the moment of purchase should at least agree to send it to you. The fee and shipping together should be under $20.

Desktop vs. Laptop

Desktop computers, the kind that have the computer sitting under or nearby the monitor, are less expensive than laptops. With a laptop, you're paying for miniaturization. A tower is like a desktop turned on its side. You can add peripherals, like a modem (to send faxes) and sound cards (to add sound), to both a desktop and a tower more easily than to a laptop.

A laptop is the better choice if you travel a lot or plan to take your computer to meetings or to the library. If you have any sense that you might eventually need a laptop, then that's what you should buy. Now that the screens have been improved and the battery life is fairly long, they're definitely comparable to desktops in terms of ease and reliability of operation. Also, access to wireless services such as two-way paging and the Internet is becoming less and less expensive. With a laptop, these options are available to you when you are away from home base.

A docking station combines the advantages of both desktop and laptop. If you and your computer are both commuters, this is your best option. With a docking-station setup, you simply slide your laptop into a bay (a larger box), and it works in tandem with the larger monitor and regular keyboard of a desktop system. The laptop is easily inserted and ejected, and you save time because you don't have to fiddle around with cables.

Suggestions when buying laptops:

- **Buy a new, brand-name laptop.** Since all laptops use unique parts, you may have a problem repairing a used laptop or a little-known brand in a situation where there are few or no local sources for replacement parts.
- **Take the service contract.** Because laptops are moved about, they are very likely to be damaged or dropped.
- **Get insurance coverage for your laptop.** Your homeowner's policy or office insurance may cover theft of a desktop computer but not theft of your laptop, especially if it's stolen while you are away from the insured premises. Laptops have the dubious honor of being number one on the list of stolen equipment. A rider to your normal insurance that covers damage or loss to your laptop should cost under $100 per year.
- **Buy a high-quality laptop bag,** like a Targa, with sturdy handles and stitching. Useful feature: a Velcro strap that fastens across the top of the laptop and prevents it from falling out in case you forget to zip the bag closed.

Comparing Features

A few years ago, computer quality varied greatly. By now, however, the manufacturers who were producing the second-rate clones have, for the most part, gone out of business, and virtually all of the companies remaining are reputable and reliable.

In the past, computers also varied widely in terms of other factors, such as speed (megahertz), hard-drive size, and video options, to name a few. That, too, is no longer the case.

The average person supposedly uses 10 percent of his personal brain power—and an even smaller percentage of his computer's brain power. Why pay for the top of the line if a midperformance machine will be adequate? That's why we say that when you shop around, you can start at the bottom. The latest model at almost any level will most likely give you more power and speed than you'll ever use.

Just FYI, here's a quick rundown of features.

Speed: Most computer manufacturers market their computers' performance based on the megahertz, or clock speed, of the computer. This refers to the number of operations, or cycles per second, that can be handled by the CPU, also called the processor. The CPU is the brain of the machine, the biggest chip in the computer, the place where the math is done and from which the information flows in and out. Intel, the world's biggest supplier, supplies the majority of the chips to Windows-based computer manufacturers. Motorola makes processors for Macs. There aren't many companies involved in manufacturing chips, so there isn't a huge variation in quality. You don't have to comparison shop.

Computers with higher megahertz numbers aren't faster enough to justify their additional cost. Besides, to the average user, this measure is irrelevant. Speed counts if you're a student of molecular fluid dynamics, but if you're using your computer to type letters in your word-processing program, the only speed that matters is how fast you can type.

The video card also affects the speed in a meaningful way. In order for you to see anything—even a letter—your computer has to draw it. Drawings are controlled by the video card, or the circuit board, that converts computer signals into TV pictures. The faster your computer can draw, the faster it can run. Video cards range in price from under $100, which is adequate for the average user, to a couple of thousand dollars. If you run games with complicated graphics in Windows or newer Macs, spending a couple of hundred dollars might be worth it. (The early Macintoshes have built-in video cards and can't be upgraded). The upgrade doesn't double the speed of the overall computer—it doubles the speed at which images appear on the screen.

RAM: RAM is short-term memory. Short-term memory is used to handle everything you're working on at any given moment. The more RAM you have, the more applications you can run at the same time. Extra RAM increases the speed

at which you can work, because you can go back and forth between applications rather than having to close one down to use another, but it doesn't increase the speed of the computer. In the past, machines usually didn't come with enough RAM, but today most computers come with thirty-two to sixty-four megabytes (MB). Thirty-two should be enough for a typical individual user.

Hard drive: This is long-term storage capacity—how much you can load and keep on your machine. It's not a basis for comparison, because all the newest machines have more hard-drive capacity than you're ever likely to need. If you manage to fill it up, you're probably ready for a new machine anyway. More likely, you need to clean out the machine and dispose of files that are the computer equivalents of odd socks and back issues of magazines you will never read.

Bundled software: This is software that comes packaged with your computer. It meets the usual standard for stuff you get free—in other words, most of it will be useless and you'll probably want better quality in the rest. There are some exceptions, though. For example, you might get Microsoft Word or Office, or another program that would cost a couple of hundred dollars, as part of your bundle. But don't buy a computer on the basis of free software.

Other considerations: Try out any computer you're thinking of buying. How comfortable does the mouse feel? How heavy is the laptop? Ask around. Read product reviews in the computer magazines—if a machine gets a couple of five-star reviews, it's worth considering. Don't get an opinion from someone who's doing wind-tunnel research if your needs are a lot less complicated. (If you were looking for a station wagon, would you check with James Bond?) Check with friends whose needs for the machine are similar to yours.

Don't buy anything that's the latest and greatest until it's been out for six months to a year and the bugs have been worked out. Just ask all those folks who wanted to be the first on the block to own the Edsel, the worst car-manufacturing mistake ever made.

That comparison came to mind because, as it turns out, computer manufacturers are taking a page from the car manufacturers' books and giving their new models exotic names and weird-looking cases. However, computers that call attention to themselves on the basis of their looks are strictly for the reception desks at hip advertising agencies. Even if they do perform well despite their bimbo exteriors, if you accidentally crack the cover on these nonstandard computers, you will have to get the part direct from the manufacturer, which is costly and time consuming.

Don't be seduced by a brand name. When a company becomes successful and sells a ton of machines, it may begin to have problems keeping up with demand. Sooner or later, some part of the system breaks down and the company may start using cheaper components. A manufacturer that made a great machine three years ago could be making garbage today.

Price: You'll pay extra for additional RAM, a bigger hard drive, a larger monitor, a faster modem, a fancier keyboard, a three-button mouse, an extra battery for a laptop. If the company is spending a load of money on advertising, that ups the price, too. Some people like to boast that they've paid more money for their machine, but that doesn't make it any better. You don't buy a computer the way you buy a refrigerator, expecting it to last for twenty years. A computer is a short-term purchase. Ask yourself how much you are willing to pay for a machine that you may replace in two years.

The latest and greatest development in computers was what the industry calls the "sub-$1,000" computer—that is, a basic model costing less than a thousand dollars. Add an additional $500, and you can have the whole setup including not only the computer, keyboard, and monitor, but also a printer, modem (which connects you to the Internet), and some preinstalled software. Well-known brands come with better-quality software, but all of the sub-$1,000s come with some sort of word-processing program that allows you to write documents, as well as a spreadsheet program that lets you do accounting and charts. And all of them are "plug and play"—that is, they are ready to operate the minute you get them home, which may seduce you into failing to read the manual (despite the fact that you really should).

Now that the $1,000 barrier has been broken, even cheaper machines are appearing. But listen up: Sometime along the way, you're going to need service—tech support on the phone, repair service on the machine—and compa-

nies just don't make enough profit to invest a lot of service in a machine that they're selling really, really cheap. When you have a problem, solving it may cost you more than you would have spent on a better-quality machine.

In the end, the most critical factor in choosing the "best" computer isn't the machinery but the kind of backup you're going to get.

The Deciding Factor: Service and Support

When people are looking for a new computer, the last thing on their minds is what will happen when the new machine crashes. But no matter how much you love your new computer, you may be a candidate for "Can This Marriage Be Saved?" once you make that first call for assistance.

So, the smart thing to do is see what you're in for. Good manufacturers offer extended warranties and service-plan options, plus free phone support, Web support, and sales support. Before you hand over your credit card, preview what will happen if you run into a problem.

Ask about the warranty. The warranty is a measure of the company's faith in its own product. What kind of warranty are you being offered? What will it cost to extend it? A one-year warranty is standard. A three-year warranty is gold-quality service.

Check out the service contract. Will a technician come to you, or do you have to bring the machine in when you have a problem? What do they say is the turn-around time for a repair?

Do a trial service run. If the store you may buy from offers servicing, call and say that your computer needs repair and ask how long it will take. (Does the service department give you the same kind of response that the salesperson promised?) If you're planning to buy from a catalog or over the Internet, you'll deal directly with the manufacturer. Make the same type of call.

Test drive the tech support. Make up a question, then place a call. See if tech support is one of the first options you're offered when you call. See how hard it is to get to the right place through the voice-mail system. See how long you stay on hold before you reach a live human being. See how clearly your question is answered. At press time, Dell is offering the best warranty, the best tech support, and the best prices.

The best kind of protection you can look for is a lemon clause that will cover you in case the machine is a real dud. One of our clients bought a new laptop and ran into several service problems within a year. Finally, he said, "I don't want this repaired again." (Only he said it a lot more colorfully.) He demanded a new computer in exchange. Fortunately, his warranty stated that the company would take back any machine that had three or more service problems within twelve months of purchase.

For many appliances, buying service plans isn't cost-effective. A refrigerator, for example, is designed to last a relatively long time, and the technology doesn't change much. But neither of those things is true of computers. We suggest that when an extension to your warranty is offered, take it—the cost will almost always be equal to or less than most one-time service charges. Should you fail to extend, then change your mind, you may have to have your computer checked by the company before you can re-up. If you've ever had a checkup yourself to reenter a health plan, you know what a pain that can be.

Most extended warranties are transferable, so another reason to keep your warranty current is that if you decide to sell your used computer, you'll have a valid warranty to offer the purchaser. This adds a lot to the resale value.

Buying Printers

When it comes to printers, there's every other brand and then there's Hewlett-Packard. In our opinion, HP is the one and only choice. These printers are most reliable, win top ratings all the time, and come with a wide range of features. Unless you're printing high-resolution photographs or have some other specific

printing need, just buy whichever HP model fits within your budget. Even the bottom of the line of this brand is sturdy.

Hewlett-Packard makes some machines that are compatible with both Windows and Macs. Pay whatever extra it costs to buy a printer with this feature, because it will have a lot higher resale value.

Inkjet printers give a better bang for the buck than a laser printer. They are smaller, lighter, and less expensive. Also, they can do color printing. Laser printers are faster and the print quality is better, but inkjets are closing in on them.

Service Contracts for Other Items

Monitors, printers, and laptops usually come with only a one-year warranty. This is a really big clue as to the likelihood that they will need replacement or repair. So, Sherlock, buy the service contract.

Because they run at high temperatures, monitors often blow and need replacement after about a year. A service contract will cover this possibility.

Printers may last through several computers, but will need servicing along the way. That's because they have a lot of moving parts and the ink leaves residue that clogs things up. Most aren't worth repairing unless they're under warranty. You probably couldn't even find anyone willing to repair a dot-matrix printer.

Like office copiers, laser printers use toner cartridges as the "ink." The black powder makes them dirty, they get paper jams, and they are expensive to repair. Most copier-repair shops also repair laser printers, but expect to pay a lot. A $250 bill is not uncommon. (Actually, a $250 bill would be counterfeit. But a bill *for* $250 is not uncommon.)

Don't pay to extend the warranties on any devices other than printers, monitors, and laptops. Instead, buy recognized brands from a reputable source, not cheapos at a flea market. High-end products are more likely to last longer and also come with longer warranties.

Where to Buy

Buying a computer direct from the manufacturer is a great way to go. Almost all of Dell computers are sold this way, and that has enabled the company to devote more money and resources to tech support. Now other companies, such as Compaq, Apple, and idot.com, are selling direct to consumers over the Internet. Because they have no overhead, companies who do this can offer excellent prices.

Test drive the tech-support number to make sure you're dealing with a reputable company before you order by mail or via the Web.

Another option is ordering by mail from such catalog companies as CDW (Computer Discount Warehouse), Buy.com, MacMall, and Mac Warehouse. (For more about ordering by mail, see appendix D, "Resources.")

Retailing via catalog and the Internet are part of a shift toward virtual shopping that has been helped by the fact that shipping has become cheaper and quicker. Also, because the products the different outfits offer are essentially identical, you don't have to look at them to make your decision. You just need a catalog or part number and you can get whatever you want overnight.

Still, if you buy over the Internet or via a catalog and there's something wrong with your machine, you have to ship it back where it came from.

Keep the packing box from computer equipment for six months in case you have to ship the computer back for repair. If you have discarded your packaging, most companies will send you a box to ship your computer in if you need to have it repaired. Request the box when you make arrangements for the pickup.

Though shipping may be inconvenient, it can be swift. For example, a friend with a Mac laptop problem called Apple for repair on a Thursday evening. The company arranged a late-evening pickup from her home in New York City, flew it to the West Coast, and returned it in working condition by Saturday morning. (The availability of prompt shipping service plus our technical savvy has enabled the Geek Squad to be the Rolling Stones' favorite computer-repair company. No matter where in the world they're touring, we can do a turnaround within seventy-two hours.)

Nevertheless, even with the money saved by buying by mail or the Internet, some people prefer to pay a little more and shop locally just to have someone to deal with face-to-face in the event of any service problems.

Chapter Two

PREVENTING PROBLEMS

What Makes Computers Act Weird

Computers are pretty reliable and docile machines. They don't make much noise, they don't require much upkeep, and, most of the time, they do exactly what they're supposed to. As we've mentioned before, there are only three sources for problems: something mechanical, something in the software, or something you're doing. Here's the deal:

Reasons for a physical or mechanical problem: Something is broken or not set up properly. Maybe the hard drive's motor isn't working. Maybe a screw is missing. Maybe the computer is overheating. All of these problems are relatively rare.

Reasons for a software problem: There are three layers of software in your computer:

- **Operating-system software.** It turns on the computer and keeps it running.
- **Application software.** Applications, also known as programs, let you do what you want to do with the computer. Word-processing programs let you work with words. Spreadsheet programs help you work with numbers.
- **Documents (also called files).** These are the things that you personally create using the program software—a press release or a letter to your mom, a pie chart or a summary of your August checks.

Then there's another, sort of hidden layer. The operating system of your computer can't talk directly to a printer. To do so, it needs another little piece of software that works like a translator. This piece of software is called a driver, because it "drives" the device. It's a teeny-weeny program, small enough to fit on a floppy. Each device—the scanner, printer, removable disk drive, CD-ROMs, mouse, modem, and sound card—has its own driver. You could get a computer to operate any kind of machinery—you could even get the microwave to cook your popcorn by remote, if you had microwave-driver software.

Very often, people have problems because their printer driver is not working correctly with their computer. They're trying to use an old printer with a new computer, for example, or vice versa, and the drivers aren't compatible—sort of like you trying to drive a tandem bicycle with your grandfather. Your pace and energy level aren't the same. (Read "Continue Your Computer's Education," page 52.)

All software is stored on your hard drive, and any software problem can be solved. If it's gone hopelessly bad, the solution may be to remove it—erase the operating software, the program software, and your documents from the hard drive—and then put it back. I know you're thinking, "Are you crazy? Erase my hard drive?" It seems pretty weird that removing everything and then putting it back will make it work correctly.

Think of software programs as little puppies: They're not housebroken, so as they get older, they create more problems. Similarly, as you create and delete files and modify things, they tend to leave a lot of little "mistakes" behind that the computer doesn't quite clean up, all of which slow down the system. It is in the nature of the way a computer manages and stores information that this can happen. A computer is just not a perfect housekeeper.

By erasing everything and reinstalling programs, you start over again and clear out the junk. Also, erasing and reinstalling serves another purpose. Like a move, it inspires you to get rid of unnecessary stuff. When you erase and reinstall, you are forced to rethink what you're keeping in your hard drive. People tend to install any disk they get, whether or not they use it. But while such disks may have been free, they cost you time by slowing down your machine. When you do a reinstall, try to eliminate everything but the basics: for example, word processing, a spreadsheet application, Quicken, and the Internet. When there's less to manage, the machine runs faster and better.

A complete reinstallation is simple and not risky, provided you have the three things you really need: the disks that came with the operating systems of your computer and all your devices, all the disks that came with the program software, and backup disks of all the material you personally created.

We'll tell you when to do it, and how. But first, we'd like to tell you how to prevent a problem from occurring in the first place. Note that this chapter, on preventing problems, is one of the longest in the book. If you read it and heed it, you may never have to read the rest of the book (though you may be curious to find out how it ends).

The following section explains what to use and what to do to avoid the most common mechanical and software problems or—if they do occur—prevent a computer Chernobyl.

Why Geeks Have Fewer Computer Problems

Nongeeks have better relationships with people, but geeks have better relationships with their computers. That's because geeks plan ahead. They wear scarves in the winter and pocket protectors all year round and never lose their umbrellas. And, also, they are very logical, which may not work so well with people, but is helpful in dealing with machines. If something is wrong, they do not assume that they have bad computer karma. Instead, they look for a reason. You, too, can live the relatively trouble-free geek computer life if you follow these simple rules:

- Save every single floppy disk or CD that comes with your computer and every piece of related equipment. And remember that they will do you no good if they are located in a box in the closet behind your paint-stained sneakers and the deflated basketball. Put them where you can find them. You are 100 percent guaranteed to need them again. Often, a simple solution for any problem is just to reinstall the operating system.

- Save the manuals. Even if you're the kind of person who hates manuals and mostly uses them for things like propping up a chair leg, you may be surprised at how useful they can be when you are troubleshooting. In fact, a manual may describe and solve the very problem you are having. Every computer and device has its own special quirks and capabilities, and a manual knows its machine like, well, a book.

- Be patient. For example, a computer that appears to be frozen (the mouse is not responding to your commands) may just be taking a little longer than you anticipated to get its work done. Maybe the little men inside are tired today. Sometimes just waiting a few seconds will solve the problem. Go and get a drink of water or make a phone call, and you may return to find that your machine is operating again. In any case, screaming at your computer doesn't help. Though it may speak, it cannot hear.

- Eliminate the obvious. Do not assume that the entire machine is critically ill when it may simply have a hangnail. Always try to find out whether the problem is generic or specific. If you're having a problem with a disk, try another disk. If you can't print one document, try to print another. Maybe the computer is fine and the problem is with a bad disk or a single quirky document.

- Don't install upgrades unless you know in your heart that you are a real geek and are totally confident that you know what you're doing. If you aren't, find an authorized geek to help you. (You'll know him when you see him.)

- Don't change settings unless you're absolutely certain that you know what the consequences of the change will be. For example, don't play around with the modem speed to try to make it faster. Don't change display settings to try to get more colors. Be careful when changing keyboard settings—strange things may happen. Your computer may begin speaking Swedish, or worse. And if you can't resist turning a few knobs here and there, write down what you're changing step by step, so that you can backtrack. (Geeks are excellent at this kind of detail.)

- Don't delete a file unless you're absolutely sure you don't need it. We're not referring to the files you've created yourself. We're talking about the ones you find in your operating-system and program software, files whose names you don't recognize. Deleting files is always potentially risky, so the rule of thumb is, if you don't know what it does, keep it. If you feel the need to clean house, look through the stuff you can identify.

- Don't attempt to fix a problem unless you know what it is. This applies to life as well as to computers.

Getting Along with Your Computer

Treat It Like a Dog

Your computer is as loyal to you as a dog, so why not treat it just as well? Make sure that you keep it in good condition, and don't do anything that might cause it harm. Basically, a lot of the same rules apply to both computers and dogs:

- **Clean it regularly.** A mouse should be cleaned every six months, and the computer should be cleaned once a year, especially if you're in a dusty environment. Dust acts as an insulation blanket and will trap heat, which can damage the computer. But be that as it may, don't try to put a filter on the computer—that may cause overheating and do more damage than good. Instead, once a year get compressed air in a can from a camera shop or stationery store. Spray it in any of the open areas of the disk drive, in any ventilation holes, and on any fans.

• **Give it periodic checkups:**

Windows users: The system comes with two built-in utilities, ScanDisk and DeFrag for Windows. Every two months, you should run these utilities, which perform maintenance checks on the machine. (See "Checkups" on page 59.)

Mac users: Use your built-in Disk First Aid. (See "Checkups" on page 59.)

• **Avoid secondhand smoke.** It can be lethal to computers as well as to living things. Tiny tar-containing particles from smoke easily find their way inside your computer, where they can do a lot of harm. For example, CD-ROMs use very small lasers. When these are coated by smoke particles, which is common in homes with heavy smokers, the drives may malfunction.

• **Be gentle.** Don't hit, knock, rock, or otherwise disturb your machine, particularly when it's turned on. The hard-disk drive inside is spinning at thousands of rpm. If it's jostled, data can be damaged or lost.

• **Don't leave your computer (or your dog) in a hot car with the windows closed.** Don't expose it to extremes of cold, either. If a computer gets too hot or cold, it will start to malfunction and lock up. If for some reason it is exposed to extreme temperatures, your computer (or any electronic device, for that matter) should not be turned on immediately. Give it an hour to return to room temperature. Also, avoid direct sunlight, and damp, moist environments.

• **Keep it on a short leash.** When you connect your Mac to a printer or other device, avoid using four- and five-foot cables. Use shorter ones, because the farther a signal travels, the greater the likelihood that it will be degraded.

Deal with Power Issues

• Peripherals (devices) should be the first items on and the last items off. For example, first turn on the printer and scanner, and then turn on the computer. Shut the computer off, then turn off the devices. When you issue a command, such as "print," the device should be ready to go. If it's not on,

you may get an error message that will delay operations. Similarly, if you have forgotten that one or more of the peripherals is still operating, when you try to shut the machine down, there will also be a delay.

- Always use the Shut Down commands to turn your computer off. If you just cut the power without shutting down the machine, you can damage your hard drive or mess up the contents of important files. This is true of every computer system ever produced.
- When you turn off the machine, do not try to restart it immediately. Wait at least ten seconds. The hard drive needs time to spin down, among other things.
- Use a surge protector or uninterruptible power supply (UPS) to moderate the power supply. Especially in older communities, you may get "dirty," or fluctuating, power. A surge of too much power can fry the components of your computer or any other electronic device (and wreck both the data and the hardware), and a sudden loss of power may cause a reboot and data loss. The point of a surge protector is to keep the power supply consistent.

Counting on an inexpensive surge protector, though, is like relying on a telephone psychic to warn you that trouble is on the way. A good one costs between $40 and $100 and has a UL (Underwriters' Laboratory) standard of 1449. (You should be able to find this information right on the package.) Otherwise, it's just an extension cord. If you want complete protection, you need an uninterruptible power supply. A UPS is basically a battery that comes to the rescue when it's needed, and can cost anywhere from $120 to thousands of dollars. The higher the price, the longer it will provide power to your computer in the event of an outage. A typical user would probably be fine with a $120 model, which could keep you going for around five minutes—enough time to close your documents and shut the machine down properly.

Do you need to invest in a UPS? In the event of a power problem, you'll typically lose only material that hasn't been saved. If you save often, this wouldn't be much of a predicament. But if you work on a network server, others on the network could be updating material at any moment. During even a brief outage, a lot of information could be lost, so in such cases you need a UPS.

• Do not turn the machine on and off with the surge protector. That defeats the purpose of the protector, which is to absorb any kind of power problem before it gets to your machine.

• An electrical storm can do damage to your computer even if it is turned off. Although this sounds like something Stephen King might have dreamed up (electrical force attacks machine), it happens fairly often. So, if a thunderstorm is threatening, unplug your computer from the wall or from the surge protector.

• If stormy weather is forecast, unplug the telephone cable from the modem, too. Modems are often destroyed when lightning strikes telephone poles.

• To protect your modem, buy a surge protector with a telephone jack.

Obey the Twelve Commandments

1. Treat your disks carefully.

• Don't turn on a machine with a CD-ROM or floppy inside.

• When inserting a disk, make sure that you've got the right side turned up. Also, be sure that the sliding metal portion is not bent upward. If it is, the disk may get stuck when you try to eject it.

• Remove any Post-it notes before you insert the floppy. The port is designed to take a floppy of a precise thickness. A disk decorated with a Post-it might cause it to jam up.

• If a CD (or disk) doesn't slide easily into the port, consider the possibility that one is already there. Many people just keep trying to jam the second one in. Then they bring the computer to us for repair.

2. Be sensible when connecting and disconnecting cables.

• Don't use frayed or otherwise damaged cables.

• Hold the cable by the connector (the plug), not by the cord.

• Make sure that the connector (plug) matches the port and that it's right

side up. If connector and plug don't join easily, you're probably not matching the right connector with the right port.

3. Be careful when you travel.
- Keep a laptop in the sleep mode or turned off when you're traveling. If you shake up the hard drive, you can do a lot of damage.
- Don't transport a machine with a floppy disk in place.

4. Cover up. A lot of computers have expansion slots in the rear. After installing an upgrade, people often forget to replace the cover, leaving the computer exposed to dust. If you see any open spaces in the back of your computer, have them dusted out and the slots covered when you take it in for maintenance. (If the cover is misplaced, take your computer to a computer store, and we bet you will find a nice person to give you a cover.)

5. Don't cover up. Don't place books, files, the box from your cheeseburger, or anything else on top of the monitor vents. These allow air to circulate and permit the monitor to cool. If they're blocked, you risk a fire and/or damage to the computer.

6. Don't put the computer on or near speakers, large color televisions, or any other device emitting large amounts of electromagnetic waves. (Refrigerator magnets aren't a problem, although many of them look pretty cheesy.)

7. Never, ever place a laptop on the corner of a desk. This is not a *feng shui* thing. There is nothing about computers and corners that is cosmically incompatible. But things placed on the corners of desks tend to get knocked off.

8. Don't play percussion on the keyboard.

9. Keep foreign objects out of the disk drive. We can understand how a bean could wind up in an ear, but that narrow little slot in your computer just doesn't seem particularly inviting. So we have long wondered why we had to service a CD-ROM drive stuffed with a chocolate-chip cookie. (Feeling fondly toward his computer, he decided to reward it with a treat?)

10. Your CD-ROM tray is not a cup holder.

11. Do not attempt to control your mouse with anything other than your hand. (Or your mind.) You'd be amazed at how many people try to use their feet—unless you're one of them.

12. Keep liquids away from the computer.

LIVING ON THE EDGE (or, Don't Use Liquids Around Your Computer)

Sitting at my computer,
holding my
poised and curved fingers
over the virgin
and vulnerable
electronic
keyboard
beneath—
to my right,
sharing my mousepad,
a full can of diet ginger ale
and a glass filled with ice and a straw,
and to my left, a small cup
with leftover Coke
still sitting from the night before last—
I feel like a
stunt man at MGM,
alternating
between
Ford and Willis;
the first man out on a parachute jump
over shark-infested
Caribbean waters;
an Outward Bound climber
broaching Annapurna's summit
alone,
oxygen tanks left at the base camp;
the top rider on a fire engine
in Chicago of 1871.
Now you may say,
why do you live on the edge?
Just the old daredevil
in me.

—Martha Rose Reeves

General Software Smarts

Keep Your Startup Disks

We've already said that you must keep your disks, but it's important enough to repeat. The floppies or the CD-ROMs containing the operating system(s) for the computer, the printer, keyboard, and every other device you own should be stored safely away in a cool, dry place. In case of a problem, the most common solution is to reinstall the operating system or application—and for this you need the original disks. You can't work from copies.

If the systems came preinstalled in your computer, try to get the disks. (See "Buying a Used Computer," page 25.)

Even if you have the originals, follow the instructions in the manual for making another set of operating disks as a precautionary measure and store all your disks in a safe place off-site. (For more on this, see "Keep It Simple," page 57.)

Backup disks should be stored in a place that you can remember to look in when you need them. The storage area should be cool and dry, and if you're really concerned about safety, it should be off-site.

Organize, Organize, Organize

Giving advice about organizing files is like giving advice about what kind of underwear you should buy. Everyone is comfortable with a different style. But there are a couple of things to keep in mind:

- Put things where you are most likely to find them. Only you know how your brain works (at least you're ahead of anyone else in this department), so organize your files accordingly. Give your files names that make sense to you.
- Put all the items relevant to a particular topic in the same place. This is not just to keep things tidy, but also to safeguard the material. If something goes wrong and you have to reinstall operating systems or applications, you may inadvertently delete something that has not been put with other related documents.

• Windows 95/98 users: Do not tamper with the extension names—the letters that follow the dot when you name files in certain programs. The letters help your computer pull up the appropriate software when you want to access those files.

Here's how to get started:

Mac users:

1. Go to the desktop, select New Folder from the File menu, and name the folder "Documents." Continue to step 2, below.

 **Mac users:** If you've got a long list of items in a window, and you want to select most of them but not all, first press Command+A (which selects all of them), and then hold down the Shift key and click the items you do NOT want to move, unhighlighting them. Then you can move all of the highlighted ones at once.

Windows users:

1. If you don't find My Folder on the desktop, then create a folder called "My Files" to store your documents. Continue to step 2.

2. Open the folder, and create new folders within it to hold everything you've created. Give each folder a name, such as "Correspondence," "e-mail," "Finances," "Internet Downloads," and so on. Drag each of your individual documents into the appropriate folder. Once you get the hang of it, you'll find that everything you've got fits into a limited number of categories. It's OK to mix two types of documents that relate to one another in a single folder. In other words, you can put both your Excel spreadsheet and a letter to your accountant in your Finances file, because most computers can tell the difference between a spreadsheet and a word-processing document. When you double click on the item you want, it shows up on your screen.

Again: Never get rid of a file if you're not sure what it does. But don't load the computer like an attic, with stuff you're afraid to get rid of, either.

134 MEGABYTES AND GROWING

There is one miracle on the computer

that often goes unappreciated.

Everyone notices

its speed,

the Internet,

the World Wide Web,

and no one

no one ever mentions

the trash—

the trash can that can take and take and take and never be too full.

A reluctance to throw anything out

can unfortunately carry over to

the computer.

Take

me,

for

instance.

I have a particular reluctance to

throw things

out,

and as a result,

even when I finally go to empty my computer trash

it says

things like, "The trash contains thirty-five items, which use

415 KB of disk space.

Are you sure you want to permanently remove these items?"

and I cringe and tend to pause.

Who wouldn't?

"Permanently remove."

If only it would say

something

more middle of the road

like,

"No doubt you've considered removing this trash for some time now

and if you are fairly comfortable with the idea that you

won't be using these items

you might as well

discard them

and

have a good day."

But no:

the

dialogue box

makes me feel like

an executioner,

and as a result,

the contents of my trash are now

165 items, 134 MB of disk space

and growing

—*Martha Rose Reeves*

Continue Your Computer's Education

Your printer, your scanner, your monitor, your word processing, and other parts of your computer setup may all come from different software and hardware manufacturers. These people can't test their products in every possible combination, so they rely on customer feedback to find out how they're doing. If, for instance, someone reports that using a Hewlett-Packard printer with another brand of scanner creates a particular kind of problem, the engineers at Hewlett-Packard figure out how they can modify the printer's operating-system software to make it compatible with the scanner. Periodically, they release updates for the printer driver that incorporate all the modifications.

Your job is to make sure that your hardware has the latest and greatest modifications so that everything works in sync. Fortunately, this is usually done very easily via the Internet. Go to the device manufacturer's, not computer manufacturer's, Web page (if you're using a Hewlett-Packard printer with your Mac, go to HP, not Apple); most have one. Click on the "driver update" section. Installing the updates, which are free, is just a matter of pointing and clicking.

How often should you visit? Unless you're a real technophile who enjoys checking out every nuance, visiting too often will probably just confuse you. While bugs may be reported and corrected twice a week, changes will actually be incorporated only into periodic updates, so probably once or twice a year is enough. On the other hand, if you change something, and particularly if after the change you're having problems—the printer isn't working as well since you added a digital camera—now's the time to do an update.

Don't Be a Guinea Pig

Companies that produce hardware and software may release something called a "beta version" of their products. A beta is supposedly workable, but hasn't yet been field tested—it may still contain some kinks. The companies provide this version free to impulsive people who are willing to act as guinea pigs. The beta crowd then discovers the bugs in the system in the worst possible way—by experiencing crashes that go right off the Richter scale. Unless you are the kind of person who might enjoy walking through a minefield, leave the beta testing to other people.

Backup Basics

The worst consequence of a crash, or any kind of computer problem, is not the cost of the repair or of replacing the parts. It's not even being without a machine. You can always get a loaner or establish temporary headquarters at Kinko's. The catastrophe is losing your data. Frantic people arrive at our office on a regular basis, terrified about having lost forever what was in their machine. Sometimes they have. Some of the world's greatest novels may have disappeared into nothingness because the writer didn't back up data.

Preparation is the best defense against a crash, but people are lazy about preventive measures. This is great for our business, but terrible for the people. The sad part is that prevention is quick, easy, and very inexpensive—especially when compared to the cost of a new computer and/or professional data recovery. Some prevention costs nothing but time.

Safeguarding your files

Backing up is like exercising or eating vegetables. Everyone knows that it's good for you, but a lot of people don't do it. Or they do it sometimes. This a way of living on the edge, though not in an interesting, obscure-rock-group kind of way. Once you learn to depend on a computer, you will come to rely on it to keep track of an ever-expanding amount of material, from financial records and home-business information to the Christmas-card list and daily calendar. If there is a crash, all this can be permanently lost. A mechanical problem can be almost as devastating as a fire or a flood in your house.

One way to save yourself lots of grief is to save regularly as you work. In the Preferences section of your word-processing program, you will find features that can help you. You can select intervals at which the machine will do an Automatic Save or Background Save. Or you may prefer to be prompted instead of having saves done automatically; for instructions on doing this, check your manual. As an additional safety feature, in the Save box of your word processing, when you create a new file, you will probably also find another box that says "Make Backup." If you choose this option, when you change the original file, changes are made to the backup, but only after a brief interval. So if you inadvertently erase something, you can act immediately to retrieve it from your backup file.

Even if you succeed in rescuing all or part of the data by one means or another, it may cost you a lot of money and time. The hours you spend creating files are much more valuable than the cost of the computer. If you have a proper backup strategy, when Rover sends your computer crashing with a wag of his tail, you may have to replace the machine, but in any case you will be able to take your backup disks to a business center or a friend's house and keep working.

Always make a current backup before installing new software on your computer. New software has been known to cause crashes during installation.

Choose the Right System

A *floppy disk* is the most basic backup system. Up to two megabytes of documents will fit on a floppy, and floppies are cheap. (The original "floppy" disks were so named because they were pliable. The ones commonly used today are called "floppies"—and, more accurately, diskettes, microfloppies, or 3.5-inch disks—only to distinguish them from the "hard disk," or hard drive, that is inside your machine.)

Floppies are fine for moving a particular document from one machine to another, but they aren't reliable for long-term storage. They aren't hermetically sealed, so they can go bad—victims of humidity or dust or an overturned cup of coffee. Usually, you won't realize the disk is bad until you insert it into the computer and see the words "Disk error" or "Disk cannot be read" or a similar message that can ruin an otherwise ideal day. Many people routinely use one particular floppy to back up a spreadsheet or a daily reminder and learn a lesson in betrayal when it goes sour on them.

Trust no disk. If you're using the computer daily, use five different floppies on

a rotation of Monday to Friday (extras, obviously, if you work on the weekend) and just keep cycling through them. If any one of them dies, at least you're up to date through yesterday. If the idea of losing a whole day's work makes you faint, then back up more often. You can be as cautious or obsessive as you want.

Every three months, toss out all your floppies (and tapes and diskettes for removable storage systems, as described below) and start with fresh ones. This is cheap insurance against data loss.

Bottom line on all of this: Floppies are fair-weather friends that can let you down at any moment. Protect yourself by making multiple copies.

Here's an organizing tip if you're backing up on a floppy: When you're quitting for the day, use the date selection on the Find File feature to locate all the files you may have worked on or changed that particular day. Copy all of them onto your floppy.

At some point you may outgrow the floppy backup. Once you have accumulated documents in excess of 1.4MB, you will need a second floppy. Eventually, you'll need three, four, and even more to copy your material. Before this happens, upgrade to a removable drive.

A *removable storage device* uses diskettes that have the convenience of a floppy—they are easily inserted and removed, and you can transport them in your pocket—plus they can hold many times more information. If you're an average user, and if you keep your documents in a single folder that you can drag onto the disk, you can back up a huge amount of material in less than three minutes. (While you're waiting, boil yourself an egg.)

There are several brands of removable storage devices. The Geek Squad likes Iomega, which is the pacesetter for the removable disk industry. Its Zip drive, disks for which hold about 100MB, costs about $120, while its Jaz drives are bigger (one or two gigabytes) and more expensive ($300 to $500). Both are easy to use and easy to install. When you're getting ready to buy, read new product reviews and ask geek-type friends to recommend what's hot right now. (If you don't have any geek-type friends, cultivate some. Hang around electronics fairs.)

Diskettes for removable drives cost about $15 apiece. If you're a normal person (and even if you're not, but you're writing a normal amount), three to five in rotation should do you fine. Unless you're living in an igloo or a furnace room, the floppies should last a couple of years, but, personally, we would play it safe and never keep them more than three months if you're doing daily back-ups. See the preceding section on floppy disks to see how to protect yourself against damaged or corrupted disks. For long-term storage, you need a record-able CD-ROM drive, which we will discuss in a moment.

A *tape drive*, which costs between $200 and $400, is a necessary evil for large organizations because of its large capacity. Small companies and individual users should avoid these things like the plague. They're difficult to set up. They're slow: a three-minute job on a removable drive would take ten minutes on a tape drive. They go bad. They break. (See the section on floppy disks for precautions.) And they're very susceptible to error.

Worst of all, you need special software to read back the recovered data. If you lose the software, you've lost all your information. And tape drives aren't in-terchangeable, so you can't play the tape from one machine on someone else's tape drive.

Tapes are often the source of major disasters in file restoration. Unfortu-nately, most people who use tape drives don't fully understand the risks and problems they present.

A final backup medium is the CD-ROM. Most CD-ROMs can only read compact disks, but with a *recordable CD-ROM system*, you can write information onto a compact disk. Generally, this system is used in conjunction with a more frequent backup system like a removable drive. If you have a lot of data and need very secure backup, this is a great choice. It's hands down the best for archival purposes.

True, it takes a little effort to set up and will set you back about $400. But the backup is quick, the recordable CD-ROMs are inexpensive, and because the system is not magnetic, the CDs are as stable as Clint Eastwood. The companies who produce them claim that this backup will last a lifetime. It's certainly good for fifteen to twenty years if stored properly—at room temper-ature and in its case, not under the seat of your '67 Nova along with Dorito dust.

Another plus is that this system is standardized. In other words, you don't need special equipment to read it. After a crash, with a CD-ROM backup, you

can simply head for a business center or a friend's house, pop the disk into any machine and keep going like the Energizer bunny.

Finally, this system will be around for the foreseeable future. While the software for your removable drive system may become obsolete within a couple of years, that won't happen with a CD-ROM backup.

CD-ROM disks are not reusable, but they cost only a couple of dollars. If you've got a particular project—say, a book like this one—you can burn all your drafts into a single CD and know that it's safe for a long while. At the Geek Squad, we use CDs for any material we want to keep for at least five years.

Keep It Simple

If people complain that a backup takes too long, that's a big clue that they're backing up too much. Maybe they don't know the difference between a full backup and a routine backup.

A *full backup* is a copy of everything in your computer—the operating systems of the computer and other devices, any applications you have installed, and documents you have created. A *routine backup* is a backup of only the documents you have created. Even if you are more fruitful and creative than Leonardo da Vinci, your entire life's work will probably be a very small amount compared to all the material involved in a full backup, so a routine backup should take very little time.

Though you will need the original disks or CD-ROMs to reinstall the applications and the operating systems for the computer and the devices after a crash, as we mentioned, disks from a full backup will recall how you or your technician customized them in various ways affecting everything from how your desktop looks to the width of the margins on your documents. You may also have added fonts, sounds, and so on. With the backup disks, you can re-create a setup identical to whatever you had before the crash. This reduces post-traumatic stress.

If you're a belt-and-suspenders kind of person, make two complete full backups and store one of the copies off-site. A safe deposit box is a good place to do so, but a friend's house is probably better because it's accessible day or night. (Well, it is if you choose a really good friend—someone willing to be awakened in the middle of the night in case of an emergency and who defines "emergency" the same way you do.) Don't bother to repeat the full backup for a year or so unless you make major changes.

 If you don't want to depend on a friend (or if you don't have any friends), you may want to store your backups with a company that sends you mailers for returning your backup tapes and disks on a regular basis. Or, you can use one of the Internet backup services. These companies use their software to get your data automatically, via modem. You can retrieve what you need by modem as well. Some of the companies will even put your data on a CD-ROM and mail it to you periodically. To keep the material secure, make sure that the company has password protection and encryption. Check the Web for the names of these services. Try Offsite Data Management Services (www.odms.com), Connected Online Backup (www.connected.com), and Mailsafe (www.ms-offsite.com).

No matter what, you should make a routine backup after every day's work—or even more frequently, depending on how much time you spend at your computer. If your files are in a single folder, as we suggest, backup is a piece of cake. Just drag the single folder over to your backup system and while it's doing its thing, you can go off and have a cup of coffee. If you organize your files so that you can do a backup this easily, you'll save time. And you'll probably be more inclined to do it regularly.

Run Practice Drills

What's the point of having a backup system if you don't know how to use it? The main purpose of a backup is to get up and running immediately in the event of a crash without having to wait for help. Once every week or two—certainly at least once a month—pretend that your hard drive has gone, and try to recover a file from whatever backup system you're using.

Keep the Backup Safe

Keep your disks, tapes, and CDs—backup or not—away from sunlight, at room temperature, and in a place where there is little moisture. Do not trans-

port a disk in your pocket or any other place where it can pick up dust, lint, a stray Raisinet, or any other alien object that might destroy information.

Preventive Procedures

Checkups

If your machine seems a little under the weather—it freezes, the printer acts up, or anything else weird or even just out of the ordinary is happening—find out where the problem is by running a disk-utility program that scans your hard drive. If the problem is a file or two in need of repair, the disk-utility program will find, diagnose, and correct it.

ScanDisk and DeFrag come with PCs; Disk First Aid comes with Macs. These do pretty low-level checkups, like an HMO clinic. If you want the equivalent of a top-notch private doc, spend about $60 on a program that does a more comprehensive check, such as CheckIt for Windows and TechTool for Macs, and Norton Utilities for both. But before you go out and spend the money, give your preinstalled disk utility a whirl. Here's how.

Mac users: Look for Disk First Aid on your Disk Tools or Utilities Disk. If you're having trouble starting the machine normally, insert the Disk Tools/Utilities Disk or your emergency boot disk. Launch Disk First Aid | Drive | Open | Repair Automatically | Start. You'll get a message telling you whether the repair was successful or not.

Disk First Aid may fail on the first attempt. Don't give up. Run it a second time, and a third and fourth time if necessary. If ultimately it fails, then run Norton Utilities. If that fails, see chapter 25, "Getting the Best Service."

Windows 3.X users: You need to exit Windows and go to DOS. At the DOS prompt, type ScanDisk, and follow the prompts.

Windows 95/98 users: ScanDisk is included with your software. If you can turn the machine on and it operates, but you have problems—you're getting messages such as "File not read," files are disappearing, text is getting garbled in a word-processing document—run ScanDisk. Pull down

Start, then click Programs | Accessories | System Tools | ScanDisk, and follow the prompts.

All Windows users: If you haven't run Surface Scan (it's one of the features of ScanDisk) within the last six months, do it now.

CAUTION: Beware of programs that claim to "prevent crashes" and "solve computer conflicts." These "miracle" programs are running on the very computer where the problem exists, so you're asking a sick computer to diagnose itself. The information you get will be oversimplified or flawed. Instead, stick with a brand-name utility such as Norton, which has its own operating system.

Vaccinations

Install software to protect your computer from a virus. Viruses are spread over the Net or through an exchange of floppy disks. When people deliberately set out to spread a virus, they often do it via the Net, baiting the unsuspecting person to click onto an infected site by advertising it with a phrase like, "Win a holiday." Still, most of the viruses that we see come through floppies.

A virus is a small program that infects the host and, like a real virus, spreads by making copies of itself. If you put a floppy with a virus into your machine, the virus, if so configured, will copy itself onto your hard drive

Computer virus

and infect existing files as well as every subsequent floppy. Antivirus software will warn that a virus is present in a floppy and ask if you want to remove it. Most of the time, this can be done without removing data.

Most viruses aren't destructive; they're just annoying. For example, a common virus will prevent you from using your floppy drive or give you a funny message. They're created by kids who have outgrown prank phone calls and are looking for a more sophisticated way to be annoying.

Viruses are like bad breath. People who have the problem often have no clue that they do. But since viruses are so widespread, they're hard to avoid. Virtu-

ally all the machines in any public place—such as a business center like Kinko's or a library or a campus computer center—have them. These machines are easy: they'll accept a disk from anyone. And no matter how vigilant the managers of these operations are, they can't be expected to run antivirus software after every new "visitor." Even though viruses are unlikely to destroy data, you should take preventive measures against them.

McAfee VirusScan (PCs) and Virex (Macs) are considered the best antivirus programs. You can get free trial versions over the Net from www.mcafee.com and www.virex.com, and you're obliged to pay for them after thirty days. (The cost is about $50.)

Antivirus software comes with a database file that includes a list of known viruses, where they come from, and how to get rid of them. If the database doesn't include the newest viruses, the program is ineffective. Since five to ten new viruses show up every week (many come from other countries or from university campuses), the software that served you well in April may not protect you in May. Monthly, or in alternate months, you should update your software. Fortunately, this doesn't cost you a penny.

Every few weeks, antivirus software–program manufacturers provide updated versions of the database files via the Internet. These small files, which are usually dated, can be downloaded from the manufacturer's Web site. Your software manual will tell you how to do this. If you don't have access to the Internet, the manufacturer will ship you a free copy of an updated file if you pay the shipping costs. Every two to three years, you should install a completely new antivirus program to make sure that you're up to date.

Mac: Rebuilding the Desktop

After any crash, your System and Finder files may become corrupted. To prevent an additional crash, rebuild the Desktop once a month, which should take you a minute or two.

Some people mistakenly believe this to be a useless procedure—but it's not. Rebuilding the Desktop allows the computer to reindex and reorganize material so that it will run more efficiently.

To rebuild, hold down the Command and Option keys during startup. The prompt will ask if you're sure you want to rebuild; click on the box that says OK. You'll see a thermometer window that will disappear when the job is done. If you're using a Mac operating system earlier than 7.5.5, the Desktop will erase any comments in your files' Get Info boxes unless you rebuild the Desktop with a disk-utility program rather than with the two-key system.

EMS for a Crashed Computer

In case the computer crashes, you need an emergency boot disk (also called the emergency startup disk or recovery disk) to keep the situation under control.

An emergency boot disk is a miniature version of the operating system, a large, critical piece of software that basically runs your computer. If the computer crashes, you can probably use the emergency boot disk to get the machine up and running well enough and long enough to copy a couple of critical files before you take it in for servicing.

When you install your disk-utility program (see "Checkups" on page 59), it will ask you if you want to make an emergency boot disk and prompt you to put in a blank floppy.

Follow these directions and put the disk somewhere safe where you can find it quickly.

> NOTE: You don't have to bother with making an emergency boot disk if your new computer has come with one. The manufacturer may call it the Recovery Disk.

When you turn on your computer and insert your emergency boot disk, the computer bypasses the hard drive and starts operating right from this emergency boot disk. Once the machine is running, your disk-utility program will tell you whether you have a physical problem with your hard drive and what the problem is. At this point, copy any data that you may need, if possible. See chapter 25, "Getting the Best Service."

> **Windows users:** When the emergency boot disk comes up, you will see the letter A followed by a colon (:) on the screen. To know if your hard drive is working, type in a C followed by a colon and then hit Enter. Now if you type "DIR" you will see all the directories that are on the drive.

Chapter Three

Startup Problems

Encountering a problem at startup is a double whammy. You're ready to boogie and the machine isn't, which is a major disappointment. Then, what's more, if it's weirded out from the get-go, it's in no condition to tell you what kind of problem you're dealing with. You don't know if the hard drive is in trouble, if there's a problem with the operating-system software, if you're dealing with a virus, or if the motherboard is failing. Usually, the computer will give some clues to help you figure things out. Well, OK, the computer couldn't care less about you, but even from what's *not* happening, you can get a sense of what's wrong.

Remember, the computer is a very logical machine, which is why geeks find it so attractive. It operates in a very orderly fashion. Once it gets power, it directs that power to its various devices as they start up. Eventually, you see the first image on the screen—the happy Mac face or the Windows startup screen. After that, you see the operating system "boot up." This is the point at which the familiar startup screen says "Welcome to Macintosh" or displays the Windows logo. Eventually, your desktop appears. If you note the exact point at which the computer is having trouble, that helps you deal with the problem.

We train our Geek Squad technicians to think in the same orderly fashion as the computer. What is the first thing a computer needs to operate?

Power. Without a source of electricity, nothing can happen. So the most basic problem that you can encounter is the dead computer.

Everyone has a different way to describe a dead computer, but what they're all describing is a situation where when you flip the switch or press the startup key, nothing happens. For us to consider a computer truly dead, it has to show no sign of life at all: no sound, no video, and—most important—no power light indicator (green or red or orange).

Here's what to do when faced with apparent death:

No Power Light

First, make sure you haven't made one of the four most common Stupid Human Tricks.

Stupid Human Trick Number One: Pronouncing your computer dead when actually you haven't plugged it in. *(Duh.)* Check that the cord is pushed snugly into both the computer and the power source. If the machine is plugged in, unplug it and proceed with the rest of the check.

Stupid Human Trick Number Two: Blaming the problem on the computer when the problem is the power source. To check this, start at the wall, not at the power strip (a.k.a. the surge protector). Plug a lamp, hair dryer, or any other item that needs power into the wall outlet and see if it turns on. If not, find a new outlet for your computer.

Stupid Human Trick Number Three: Blaming the problem on the computer when the problem is the power strip. Even if its light is on, the strip may not be working. Also, some of the outlets on the power strip may be working and others may not. Use the lamp/hairdryer routine to check each outlet individually. If the problem is the power strip, replace it.

Stupid Human Trick Number Four: Thinking the computer is dead when the problem is that the monitor is turned off.

Power cord out

Power Light On, Both CPU and Monitor Are On, but You Get No Video

Once you've ruled out the Stupid Human Tricks described above, check the voltage indicator on the back of the computer, particularly if you have recently moved it. The voltage indicator is always next to where you plug in the power cord. It is usually red or black, and you will see the numbers 110 and 220. The indicator should be set to 110 (or 115) volts for usage in America, 220 in Europe. If it's set incorrectly, the computer won't turn on. If the indicator has been incorrectly turned to the wrong setting, shut off the computer, reset the switch to 110, and restart the machine. You will have saved the time and annoyance of bringing the computer in for servicing and paying the minimum service charge of $100 for someone to flip the switch.

> **Mac users:** If there is no voltage indicator switch, or the voltage indicator switch isn't the problem, the clock battery probably needs to be replaced. See "Date and Time Errors," page 69.

Having ruled out the above, check the fan. Since computers generate heat when they run, every power supply has a fan. It is either on the back of the computer, where you plug the power in, or underneath the machine. If you can't feel air coming out of the vents and/or hear anything, use a flashlight to look through the air vents and see if the blades are turning. Here's what to do in either case:

If the fan is not turning, shut down the machine to prevent the power supply from blowing out and the machine from overheating. It won't burst into flames if it overheats, but it might lock up after twenty or thirty minutes.

Try using canned air to clean the fan. Dust that gathers in the power supply fan can cause it to malfunction.

If cleaning it doesn't help and the fan is still not turning, buy a standard fan at Radio Shack. It costs about $25. Someone at Radio Shack might install it for you. If not, buy one to take to the computer-repair center. Use your social engineering skills to try to persuade someone to install it. Otherwise, since computer-repair shops don't always have fans in stock, they might automatically replace the entire power supply, which costs $100. Even if the machine is under warranty and cost isn't a factor, by identifying the problem you might get the repair done quickly. And if the fan isn't the source of the problem, you can always return it.

If the fan is turning and the monitor is turned on but you're getting no video, you've got a hardware problem. Your emergency boot disk can't help because you don't have power. (See chapter 25, "Getting the Best Service.")

> **NOTE:** Here's the good news. Since it's a power problem, chances are your hard drive is unaffected and none of your data is lost.

Mac: There's Nothing on the Desktop

If your computer is more than one year old and you have heard the startup sound ("ping") and see a desktop, but nothing is on the screen, the most likely cause is a bad clock battery. The clock battery remembers the date and time and helps the computer remember how big your hard drive is. If the battery is bad, you may appear to have lost your hard drive because the computer can't see it. It's fine, but you have to get it on the screen again. See "Date and Time Errors," page 69.

Windows: Reports "System Configuration Has Changed"

The most likely cause is a bad clock battery. See preceding section, then go to "Date and Time Errors," page 69.

Windows: Reports "Hard Drive Failure"

You may see this at startup, but it's a hard-drive problem. See "Windows: Says 'Insert System Disk,' " page 91.

Mac: Disk with Question Mark Appears

"Hello, Geek Squad? I have a disk with a question mark on my screen." This is probably the most common Mac problem. The computer is telling you that everything else in the computer works, except that it cannot find the operating system software to start up from. Here are some simple steps to try to find the exact problem.

1. Shut the machine down.
2. Disconnect all cables from the computer.
3. Reattach the power cable, keyboard cable, mouse cable, and video cable.
4. Make sure that there is no disk in the CD-ROM.

5. Restart the machine.

6. Try to back up files and data that you need.

7. Restart with the emergency boot disk.

You will be able to see if your files are intact, and the emergency boot disk will run diagnostic tests that may make the repair and tell you what to do next. If it does not, eject the disk, shut the machine down, and restart. You may be able to copy a few critical files onto the disk. Then see chapter 25, "Getting the Best Service."

Screen Not as Expected

In a normal bootup, the screen lights up and the icons for the hard drive and drivers appear on the screen. But if there is something weird about the startup— hard drives aren't showing, programs that normally load aren't loading or are reporting errors—and especially if the machine hasn't started up in a while, try checking the physical condition of the machine or any software that doesn't require rein- stalling, deleting, or changes in settings:

1. Disconnect every cord from the back of the com- puter.

2. Reconnect only the follow- ing, making sure that they're plugged in snugly: power cord (see Stupid Human Tricks Numbers Two and Three, pages 64–65), keyboard cable, mouse cable, and video cable.

Reboot your computer

Before you restart, insert your emer- gency boot disk. (You made one, right? See

"EMS for a Crashed Computer," page 62). Now restart. Here's what to do if it works and if it doesn't:

If the emergency boot disk works, your computer will bypass the hard drive and will start from the disk. You'll see if your hard drive is there and working and if your data is there.

> **Windows users:** When the emergency boot disk comes up, you will see the letter A followed by a colon (:) on the screen. To know if your hard drive is working, type in a C followed by a colon and then hit Enter. Now if you type "DIR" you will see all the directories that are on the drive.

Also, the disk-utility software on the floppy will attempt to repair the hard drive, if that's where the problem is. Once the emergency boot disk has made the repair, it will probably tell you what to do. If not, eject the disk when it's done, shut the machine down, and restart.

If there are a few critical files that you're currently working on, you may be able to copy them onto the emergency boot disk before you eject it, if there's room. But if you're continuing to have problems with the hard drive, try calling the manufacturer's help line. Explain that you have a hard-drive problem and see if you can get help. If that approach doesn't work, see chapter 25, "Getting the Best Service." Although your machine will have to go into the shop for repair, at least you'll have your data available.

If the emergency boot disk doesn't work, go to chapter 25, "Getting the Best Service."

However, if the data on your computer is more important than the computer itself and you absolutely, positively have to have that data, deal with that problem before you deal with repair. See chapter 20, "Recovering Data."

Date and Time Errors

If the computer clock forgets the date and time, reverts to a previous setting, incorrectly reports that the date and time have changed or are invalid, repeatedly displays the same date, reports some odd date of decades ago and starts saying, "I don't know what's the matter with the kids today," it is turning middle-aged. And if it has all these quirks except for the last, it has a clock-battery problem that can be solved.

Get a replacement battery at Radio Shack or a battery specialty outlet store. It should cost less than $20.

In an older Windows-based machine, the battery may be permanently affixed to the motherboard. Unless you know how to use a soldering iron, this job is best left to the pros, and labor will cost you about $100. The clock battery in Macs and newer Windows-based machines is not permanently fixed, and replacements cost under $10. If you're hesitant or butter-fingered, don't do it, but if you're comfortable popping the cover off, replacing the clock battery is a pretty simple task.

Some battery stores may even pop the computer for you if you bring it in. As you're about to buy the battery, try an Action Jackson—hand over an extra $20 and see if you can get some help.

Date and time errors

 If not, and you don't feel comfortable replacing the battery yourself, continue on to a computer-repair shop. Say that your computer is broken, and you may pay $100 or more just for a diagnosis and/or wait the standard two weeks for a repair. But if you suggest that you think you have a clock-battery problem, you may save money. Ask the charge for swapping out the old battery, or simply offer $20. (You may have to buy the battery from them, and return the other one, but you're still ahead.)

I OPENED UP THE BACK OF MY COMPUTER

(or, Ready When You Are, Houston)

Will reentry labs want the number

on my cellular extension?

Will NASA ask the boss if I can be called

up in a crunch?

I opened up the

back of my computer this A.M.

and placed in it

a new clock battery

(right brand,

right part),

grounding myself

according to directions.

I touched the middle screw on a plug along the kitchen wall,

unlatched my computer tool kit

(the medicine bag of this electronic age),

unscrewed the back,

pulled out the mystery drawer of

the lizard colored boards

and feel pretty much

ready now

to bring the men back in from space

—Martha Rose Reeves

Sad Mac Face or "Beep" Alarm

Once your computer starts up, before it starts up the hard drive, it runs a few routine checks on the system and tells you about any serious hardware errors right away. (Even in such a case, there is a good chance that your files are safe.) There are only two causes for such problems: (1) You have recently added a piece of hardware, such as a scanner, to your system. Remove it, and have the installation rechecked. Or, (2) A hardware device in your computer has failed. See chapter 25, "Getting the Best Service."

Pay attention to error diagnoses:

Mac users: You will see the sad Mac face followed by two sets of eight-digit numbers. Write these down and bring them to your technician to help get the machine repaired as quickly as possible.

Windows users: Before you see video, you may hear one long beep, followed by a specific number of short beeps. This is called the POST code, an acronym for "*Power On Self Test*." Count the number of short beeps (there should be from one to ten) and consult the following table to break the code so you can report the problem to your repair technician. (If you missed the count, it's OK to turn the machine off and turn it back on so you can listen again. You won't hurt your computer.)

NOTE: You do not need to understand what these diagnoses mean. You are just the messenger, but you will impress any nerd with your knowledge. All of these are motherboard problems, and fixing them costs about $200.

Audio Beep Errors:

1 beep: DRAM Refresh Failure

2 beeps: Parity Circuit Failure

3 beeps: Base 64K RAM Failure

4 beeps: System Timer Failure

5 beeps: Processor Failure

6 beeps: Keyboard Controller/Gate A20 Failure

7 beeps: Virtual Mode Exception Error

8 beeps: Display Memory Read/Write Failure

9 beeps: ROM BIOS Checksum Failure

10 beeps: CMOS Shutdown Register Read/Write Error

Immediate Crash: "System Error," Cursor or Screen Locks Up/Freezes, or Other Disabling Event

A crash at startup means that a crash has occurred at some point between your turning power on and having full use of the desktop.

Here's what to do:

1. Begin by checking the physical condition of the machine or any software that doesn't require any reinstallation, deletions, or changes in setting. Most of the time, this will solve the problem.
2. If you are still having problems, and you recently installed a new device or changed something on an existing one, or even if you don't remember but suspect that you may have, turn off the machine and do a minimum system startup, as described in "Minimum System Startup" on page 210.
3. If the preceding doesn't work, and the computer is still locking up, you most likely have an operating-system problem.

In that event, back up your computer, if possible. Since your drivers are off, you may be unable to do a normal backup to a CD-ROM or a removable drive, so use floppies if you must. Then, see "Reinstalling the Operating System" on page 211 or have a professional do it.

Computer Locks Up/Freezes Ten to Twenty Minutes After Startup

If the computer starts to work, then has a problem after a few minutes, the cause is probably an overheated CPU. Today's CPUs are running so fast and generate so much heat that you could quite literally fry an egg on them. Almost all the new ones have a silver-dollar-sized fan sitting on top. These fans cost about $15, so obviously you can't be guaranteed that they will last a lifetime (unless you're a fruit fly). If the fan breaks down or doesn't generate enough cooling for the CPU, the CPU will overheat and then lock up. You will probably hear a rattling sound, which confirms that the problem is with the power-supply fan or the CPU fan. (Or there is a rattlesnake somewhere in the area. Check this first.)

Test the fan theory by shutting the computer down, then turning it back on ten seconds later. If it's still hot, it will lock up immediately. Allow it to cool for an hour, then restart. If it's a heat problem, the computer may operate for another twenty, or as few as three to five, minutes before the heat makes it lock up again. If you feel comfortable peering into the computer's private parts, turn it over, remove the cover, keep fingers away, and peek inside and look for the small (about two-inch square) CPU fan. If the computer is on and it's not moving, you've got a dead fan. (And as some movie star once said, "Dead fans don't matter.") Here is another situation where you can try some Jackson action: offer your computer repairman $20 to replace the fan for you.

Chapter Four

The Stubborn RAM

Reports "Out of Memory" or "Insufficient Memory"

These messages indicate that there is a random-access memory (RAM) problem. A lot of people mistakenly interpret this report to mean that they're running out of storage space on their hard drive.

Generally, though, when a computer is having a hard-drive storage problem, it will say, "Not enough space to store" or "Unable to write to disk." If you have less than 10MB free in the hard drive—not likely with today's machines—you may get an out of memory signal and should delete whatever items you are *certain* you don't need.

However, when RAM is the problem, the solution may be as simple as restarting your computer. You may be having a memory problem because certain applications don't quit even though you exit them.

If you get these messages often, you may have too many programs running simultaneously—not necessarily two big ones, but one big one and a lot of little gadgets. Quit the ones that aren't pertinent to what you're doing. If you have too much stuff going on, even if you have a huge amount of RAM, it slows your system. (You know how you feel after a big Thanksgiving meal?) By gadgets, we mean items you may not need—such as any icon related to using a network, if you're not in a network; the control strip that shows up in the software for your video card only to provide quick access to information that you can get elsewhere; or a feature you might not use such as FindFast in Microsoft Office. Go to your startup folder and remove them.

Should that not work, install and run a memory optimization program such as RAM Doubler (Mac), MemMaker (Windows 3.X), or Quarterdeck Memory Manager (Windows). Beware, though, that this is a bandage solution. This sort of program tricks your computer into thinking that it has more memory than it does. While these programs cost less than buying and having someone install more RAM, a cheap solution is not always a reliable solution. Confucius say, "Man who plays memory trick on computer may discover that computer forgets."

A more expensive and complete solution is to add more memory to your system.

If none of the above work, try reinstalling the application. Even if you've added more RAM, the application may not be configured to use it until it's re-installed.

Mac users: If you're trying to run a program and know that you have plenty of memory but the machine is telling you "out of memory," click once on the application's icon. (Make sure you've clicked on the original program, not on an alias.) Then click File | Get Info. On the lower-right-hand corner of the info box, there are three little boxes referring to memory: suggested size, minimum size, and preferred size. Leaving the info box open, go to the Apple menu and select About This Macintosh, which will tell you how much memory you have available. If the About Mac box says that you have 16MB of RAM and 10MB are free, return to the Get Info box and tell it that you want the program to use 9MB by entering that in the preferred-size box. This is like buying a larger home for the program—unless you change it again, the application will always have more space to work in.

Chapter Five

Video Vagaries

No matter how many hours you leave an image on the screen, it won't burn in to any of the newer monitors. And laptops, which are liquid crystal, not glass tube, aren't susceptible to burn-in at all. This is not to say that screen savers don't serve a purpose—if you press the button fast enough, no one will catch you playing solitaire or checking out something naughty on the Internet.

General Weirdness

If the introductory screens are wavy or otherwise acting as if they stayed too long at a party last night, you probably have an easy-to-solve hardware problem. Try the following:

1. Check the monitor cable. Follow the cable from the rear of the monitor to the back of the computer and make sure that it is in snug and tight.

2. Check the pins at the end of the monitor cable. It's OK if some pins appear to be missing, but none of them should be broken off or bent. (They get bent if they're angry or if someone tries to insert the monitor cable incorrectly or upside down.) If even one pin is bent, you may lose video entirely. Don't try to straighten out any bent pins, since that may cause them to crack off. Take the monitor straight to a repair shop. Though in most cases the cable is permanently attached inside the computer, sometimes it is easily detached and replaced.

3. Rule out power parasites, those evil suckers. A video problem may be caused by any device that draws power (such as an air conditioner, dryer, clock, or power strip) or any item that contains a magnet (such as a fluorescent light, fan, telephone, or speaker). Move the computer away from the devices (or vice versa) and to a different outlet.

   Test any spot where you plan to locate a computer. Put a radio in the spot and tune it to the lower bands of the AM, such as 770. If you hear strange pops, static, and the like and you're not tuned to an experimental music station, find a different place for your computer.

4. If the video is still not working properly, test a different monitor with your computer. If the second monitor works fine, your monitor needs servicing. If it doesn't, the computer needs servicing. See chapter 25, "Getting the Best Service."

Rolling Screen, Static, and/or Lines; No Clear Picture

This is technically known as "improper resolution" (to distinguish it from a proper resolution, which is something you make on New Year's Day). It often

happens after someone has used the computer to play a game. Because of their graphics, games sometimes require different settings, and the machine automatically makes the change but doesn't return to the original settings afterward. (Newer games have a prompt to warn that this may happen.)

You will need to correct the settings of your video driver, starting with a minimum system startup to initiate the basic video mode that is compatible with every computer and every setting. It will ignore all of the "wrong" settings and bring up a clear picture so that you can get everything fixed. When you're done, turn the computer off, wait a couple of minutes, then restart, holding down the buttons as indicated and preceding as directed below. (See "Minimum System Startup" on page 210 for detailed instructions.)

Mac users: Hold down the Shift key the minute you turn the computer on. As soon as you hear the Macintosh startup "ping," hold down the following keys, all at the same time: Apple+Option+Control+Shift. This is a secret key command to allow you to pick the picture resolution. Choose the lowest setting, 640 × 480, then click on Restart. If you don't restart after this procedure, since you are in minimum system startup, your programs won't run because they won't be able to access certain files.

Windows 3.X users: Get ready to hold down the Shift key the moment you see "Starting MS/DOS" pop up. You will get a C prompt. You need to change to a Windows directory, and this procedure should do it: type "CD Windows," and hit Enter. Type "Setup." When the blue screen shows up, use arrow keys to highlight Display. Hit Enter. Video options will appear. Select VGA and hit Enter. Follow the on-screen instructions, then click on Restart. If you don't restart, since you're in minimum system startup, your programs won't be able to access certain files and can't run.

Windows 95/98 users: When the machine says, "Starting Windows95" or "Starting Windows98," hit F8, and a menu comes up with many options. Choose Safe Mode. Then click on the following sequence: Start | Settings | Control Panel | Display. You will see a slide bar (like a scroll bar) that says Desktop Area. Click on the bar and slide it left, toward Less. The number you want to show is 640 × 480. (These numbers refer to the pixels, the tiny bits that make up a picture. The higher the number, the more information you can show.) Under the Color Palette, select 256. (This refers to the number of colors that can be shown. The higher it is, the more realistic the color will appear.) Click OK to clear the display settings box. Click on Restart. If you don't restart, since you're in minimum system startup, your programs won't be able to access certain files and can't run.

NOTE: If the lowest setting is already chosen, and you have recently installed a new monitor on your computer, the monitor may be operating at a setting different from that of your computer. To make them compatible, you need a synch adapter. Many computer stores sell these, but there are literally dozens of different types and usually only one type will work for a specific monitor. The best source for synch adapters, whether you've got a Mac or Windows system, is Griffin Technology, (615) 255-0990. They sell only video-related equipment, and they're the ones to call if you have any kind of video problem. They have an excellent tech-support department, too.

If the above doesn't help, you have a hardware problem. See chapter 25, "Getting the Best Service."

Red-, Blue-, or Green-Tinted Screen

1. Try the basic fixes described in "General Weirdness" on page 80.
2. Degauss (demagnetize) your monitor, if it has a degauss button. This may be on the back or side or front.
3. **Mac users:** Apple knows of a recurring problem with AppleVision 15" Multi-scan color-tinted screens. Bring the monitor to an authorized dealership and they will repair it (or send it to be repaired) for free.

INTERGALACTIC COLLISIONS (or, My Monitor Tint Shift Problem)

I haven't told too many people
about this.
There are just some things
we experience
that we feel
are better kept
low profile.
But one day
my monitor began
this color shifting—
blue, green,
black.
We aren't born
knowing
about
tint shift problems,
so we figure
intergalactic collisions are
impacting screen coloring
and leave it at that
until—
three visits to the eye doctor
later—
he says maybe it's
computer eyestrain
and you whisper
conspiratorially,
"Doctor, do you have
other people
complaining that their

monitors change
colors, even blacken out
involuntarily?"
He listens
nodding sagely
and whispers back,
"Call your
manufacturer."
Which I did,
and was told
I was in a long line
of people who had
experienced
the monitor tint-shift problem.
I am
screaming that it
blacks out entirely;
is that called
a
TINT SHIFT?
But they are cool
at these complaint departments.
She asked if I wanted
a supervisor,
implying that if I did
I would be obliged to listen to
Beethoven's Ninth
twice,
and although I often enjoy
same
at that moment
the thought of a

musical cooling of my heels
dimmed my
intensity.
I relented,
found a pencil, and
took down my date of shipment
which
(not surprisingly)
passed with no arrivals
which produced
more screaming,
more threats of
Beethoven,
and finally,
a monitor
for a
little
upgrade money
plus my old one
—though they picked up the
UPS charge.
I'm calmer now,
but if a shadow
inadvertently
flickers
across my screen
I can still feel
my body
warm up.

—*Martha Rose Reeves*

Only Partial Image On-Screen

1. Adjust your monitor controls. In newer monitors, you can usually find them on the front of the monitor as a series of dials or a series of "+" and "-" buttons with which you can adjust settings. Older monitors may have adjustment settings on the back that appear as a series of dials or holes. You'll need a small, flat-head screwdriver to make the adjustments on these. Consult your owner's manual for specific details.

2. If that doesn't do the job, look to your Control Panel for a listing under "Display," "Monitors," or "Video," or something specific to the video card manufacturer. You may find additional controls that help you make the necessary adjustments.

3. If the bottom of the scroll bar (and, possibly, some of the document as well) is missing from the screen, click the box at the upper right of the title bar (the one across from the Close box). That will reposition the window so that it is entirely visible on the monitor screen.

Brightness Fluctuates

1. Take your eyes off the computer for a second and look around. Are the lights flickering? Are you experiencing a brownout? (A brownout is a drop in voltage, not a total loss of power like a blackout.) If this happens regularly, you probably need equipment that protects you from blackouts or both blackouts and brownouts—a high-quality surge protector or an uninterruptible power supply (UPS). (See "Deal with Power Issues" on page 42.)

2. If you have other power problems, such as frequent blowing of circuit breakers, there may be fluctuating, or "dirty," electricity coming into the house. Call your power company and get it to clean up its act.

3. When an old monitor is extremely dark or flashing a lot, it is suffering. Make your peace with it. Soon you won't have it to kick around anymore.

Screen Doesn't Respond to Commands

If the mouse is still responding even though nothing is happening on the screen, wait at least twenty to thirty seconds before you react. A program may simply be taking an abnormally long time to quit.

If the mouse is not responding, press the Caps Lock key or Num Lock key and see if the keyboard light turns on and off.

• If it does not, the strong indication is that there is a complete hardware lockup caused by bad hardware or bad or improperly set up hardware drivers. Shut the computer down. Restart and see if the mouse works.

• If the keyboard light turns on and off, but the mouse is still not responding, unplug the mouse and plug it back in. If that doesn't work, follow the procedures below:

> **Mac users:** If you have two programs open simultaneously, try to leave them one at a time. Hold down Apple+Option+Escape. The screen will say "Force Quit," and you should select OK. You may lose unsaved data in the program you are quitting . Save what you can from the other program, then select Restart from the Menu. If you have only one program open, just hit Apple+Option+Power and the machine will simply reboot.

> **Windows users:** Simultaneously hit Ctrl+Alt+Del This should open the Windows Close Program window, which will list all of the active tasks running in windows. If any item shows up as "[Not Responding]," highlight that item and hit the End Task button. This should stop the corrupted task and return you to Windows. If the problem persists, you will need to reinstall the operating system. (See "Reinstalling the Operating System" on page 211.)

Freezing up can be frequent or intermittent. In either case, keep track of what you were doing when it happened and what programs you were running. If you see a pattern, you can figure out whether the problem is hardware- or software-related.

Old-Monitor Problems

Over time, you may run into one or more of the following problems: screen becomes darker or blurry, ghosting (afterimages), images may move around the screen, monitor may continually misplace its glasses. (Well, OK, we were kidding about the glasses.) These are problems of old age, and there's nothing you can do except start saving up for a new monitor and think about ways to recycle the old one. (Planter stand? Picture frame?)

Chapter Six

Hard-Drive Issues

The hard drive is part of the computer's hardware, a physical device inside the machine where your data is permanently stored.

When you turn on the machine and hear no noise or a strange noise, you may have a problem in the hard drive. Here's what to do:

Mac: Hard-Drive Icon Missing

If it's not in the Finder, run Norton Utilities' Disk Doctor.

Silence

Mac users: If you've just resurrected your idle Mac from the back of your closet, you may run into this problem. In older drives, the motor that turns in the internal drive is very likely to stick when it is not regularly used. Do not even think about WD-40. Weird as it sounds, you need to knock some sense into it. We do not recommend tossing it onto the sidewalk. Instead, begin by unscrewing and removing the cover of the computer, then turn the computer on. You will hear the sound of silence. If you recognize the hard drive, whack it on the corner with the handle of a screwdriver. (A hammer is too hard.) Try this once or twice. Replace the cover.

If it works, you should be able to hear the hard drive start to spin. Get the data off it, if you can, then go get a new drive. This "repair" is only temporary and the machine will eventually fail again.

If it doesn't work, get a new drive. If you need the data recovered, see chapter 20, "Recovering Data."

Be sure to let the repair technician know that the computer hasn't been on for a while.

Windows users: If the hard drive is silent, it is probably dead and must be replaced. If you need the data recovered, see chapter 20, "Recovering Data."

Knocking

If the hard drive makes a loud knocking sound and icons don't appear on-screen, you almost certainly have a serious hardware failure. At minimum, you'll have to replace the hard drive. See chapter 25, "Getting the Best Service." If you need the data recovered, see chapter 20, "Recovering Data." You'll need a professional.

Windows: Says "Insert System Disk"

This just means that your operating system is not set up correctly. Insert an emergency boot disk (see "EMS for a Crashed Computer" on page 62) to see if you can see the hard drive.

> **Windows users:** When the emergency boot disk comes up, you will see the letter A followed by a colon (:) on the screen. To know if your hard drive is working, type in a C followed by a colon and then hit Enter. Now if you type "DIR" you will see all the directories that are on the drive. If you can see all your data, type "SYS C:" at the DOS prompt.

If you can't see your data on the hard drive, it's better not to mess around too much—that could make it more difficult for a technician to do the data recovery. You need professional help. See chapter 25, "Getting the Best Service."

Windows: Reports "Hard Drive Failure"

This message may or may not suggest a hardware failure of the hard drive. Before you get ready to pony up hundreds of dollars for repair, see if it really is a hard-drive problem. Investigate the following:

- The problem could be a bad clock battery. See "Date and Time Errors," page 69, for instructions about how to replace it.
- The BIOS (*B*asic *I*nput *O*utput *S*ystem) may not be set correctly. The BIOS is the computer's crib sheet that reminds it of the date and time and other bits of information. If you don't use the machine for a period of time, even a couple of months, this information may disappear. (You know how it goes: Use it or lose it.) A little electrical shock over the power lines might also have this effect. Turn the computer off, restart it, and follow the instructions you usually ignore—the ones that tell you to press such-and-such a key combination to enter Setup. Go through all the settings and set up whatever makes sense to you. (There will be five to ten prompts.) In

other words, if you don't know why the machine is asking you about a particular option, don't adjust it.

If this doesn't work, see chapter 25, "Getting the Best Service."

Windows: Reports "Data Error Reading Drive C"

This means that the computer can see your hard drive, but some parts of it are damaged. You need a disk utility, like Norton Disk Doctor, that will try to repair the errors on your drive. See disk-utility programs in "Checkups" on page 59.

Reports "Not Enough Space to Store" or "Unable to Write to Disk"

This means that you are running out of space on your hard drive. You could expand your hard drive. Or you could also throw out useless files.

If you're going to buy a second hard drive, buy one from the same manufacturer who made the one in your computer. The idea is to keep everything in the family. Like human family members, they may not always get along, but on the whole they tend to be more tolerant of one another than others would be.

Chapter Seven

Floppy-Disk Failures

Floppy disks are good for only one thing: temporary transport from one machine to another. They are cheaply made and sensitive critters that have allergic reactions to air and dust, which makes them too risky for long-term backup. Read more about them in chapter 2, "Preventing Problems."

 When we say sensitive, we mean really touchy-touchy. Even pressing down too hard when you write on them may damage them. Use a felt-tip pen.

Can't Read Disks from Other People's Computers

1. The most common cause is a lack of compatibility: you're trying to insert a PC disk into a Mac, or vice versa. If so, try the following. If not, move to step 2.

   Mac users: Older Macs can't read PC disks, but newer Macs with a PC Exchange control panel can. To search for this feature, pull down the Apple menu, select the Control Panel and look for PC Exchange. If it's missing, get it from your operating-system disks or get the software from Apple or an Apple-authorized dealer. Yet while newer Macintosh computers can look at PC disks, and maybe even copy them, they cannot run PC programs without additional software. In other words, if someone writes something in Microsoft Word, you can read the disk when you insert it into your computer. But if someone copies the Word program onto PC disks, your machine won't be able to run them.

   Windows users: If the problem disk is a Mac disk, you're out of luck. Your machine can't read them. (See chapter 24, "Computer-to-Computer Communication," to see how to translate.)

2. Maybe the disk itself is damaged. Try reading it with another computer, or run a disk-utility program (see "Checkups" on page 59).
3. Try a minimum system startup. (See "Minimum System Startup," page 210, for a full description.) Briefly, you start with the machine off and all devices turned off. Then, restart as follows:

   Mac users: Hold down the Shift key the minute you turn the computer on. Insert the disk. If your computer will read the disk now, copy the files from the floppy onto your hard drive. Then restart the machine.

   Windows 95/98 users: When the screen says "Starting Windows95" or "Starting Windows98," hit F8. You will see a menu come up, with many options. Choose Safe Mode. If your computer can read the disk now,

copy the files from the floppy onto your hard drive. Then restart the machine.

Windows 3.X users: When the screen says "Starting MS/DOS," hit the F5 key, which will bring you to the DOS prompt. If your computer can read the disk now, copy the files from the floppy onto your hard drive. Then restart the machine.

4. The problem may be your floppy drive. See if it can read other disks. If not, see chapter 25, "Getting the Best Service."

Can't Transfer Information to Floppy

1. Is the disk locked? If the black tab on the underside is slid into the locked position, there will be a hole in the disk. Use a pencil or other pointed object to slide the tab so that it covers the hole. That will unlock it.

   Mac users: Mac users can also insert the disk and click on it. On the left-hand side, under the information about how many items are on the disk, look for an icon of a little padlock. If you see it, eject the disk and unlock it by sliding the tab to cover the hole.

2. If the disc is unlocked, use antivirus software (see "Preventive Procedures," page 59) to check for a virus. (Some viruses will not allow you to save information to a disk.) The software will probably be able to fix the problem. You can install antivirus software after you've got the problem. Manufacturers know that you may be buying their program in response to a virus, and the instructions tell you that the installation process begins with a virus scan. Once it's in, it protects you from future viruses.

Disk Is Reportedly Full but That Seems Impossible

Do you want to have an argument with the computer, or do you want to get the job done? Just use another floppy.

Every Disk Is Locked

The clue to solving this problem is in the question itself. What is the likelihood that every disk is locked?

1. First, check whether it is, indeed, locked:

   Mac users: Click once on the file that you're trying to write to, then go into the File menu, select Get Info, and make sure that the "locked" button isn't checked. If it continues to say that the floppy is locked, go to step 2.

   Windows users: Right click the file you're trying to write to and click Properties, where it may say that the disk is locked. To unlock it, slide the black tab on the underside of the disk to the opposite position of where it currently is. If even after you do this your computer continues to say that the floppy is locked, go to step 2.

2. Try a minimum system startup (see "Minimum System Startup," page 210) to see if you have a driver/extension conflict.
3. If that doesn't work, check for a virus with your antivirus software—some viruses will not allow you to save information to a disk. The software will probably be able to fix the problem. If a virus isn't the problem, continue on to step 4.
4. Reinstall the disk driver: Boot up with the Disk First Aid utility that came with your computer and choose the Reinstall Disk Driver option. If the driver is damaged when, for example, the computer crashes and shuts down improperly, the computer may incorrectly report that disks are locked.

Can't Insert Floppy

What is with you? If you can't put it in, has it occurred to you to check if there's something in there already?

If nothing is there, make sure that you are inserting the floppy disk correctly—that is, with the silver edge facing toward the computer and the silver disk on the bottom.

If the problem persists, see chapter 25, "Getting the Best Service."

Can't Eject Floppy

Usually, the problem is that the sliding metal door on the floppy is bent and/or caught on something.

Mac users: There is a small hole below the slot where you insert the disk. Insert the end of a paper clip about two inches straight into the hole. If you push it hard enough, the floppy will be ejected. See your computer manual for an illustration of how to do it if you're still not sure. If the floppy still won't come out, don't use force. See chapter 25, "Getting the Best Service."

Windows users: There is a manual eject button. If you encounter any kind of mechanical resistance trying to eject a floppy, don't push too hard, or you may damage your floppy drive. Take the computer to a service center and have them remove the floppy. That should cost under $50.

Disk Errors on Floppy

Mac users: If you have Disk First Aid (on your Disk Tools or Utilities disk), use your Disk Tools or emergency startup disk. Select Disk First Aid, then click Drive to choose the disk that's causing trouble. Click Open | Repair Automatically | Start.

Run Disk First Aid two or three times if the repair doesn't work on the first or second try.

Windows users:

1. The problem could be with the drive, with the software, or with the disk itself. If you put the disk in and see "Disk Error," quit all programs.
2. Try other floppies to see if your computer can read them. If the problem is with a particular floppy, run a disk-utility program on the floppy to try to fix the error.
3. If this doesn't do the trick, the drive needs servicing. See chapter 25, "Getting the Best Service."

Noisy Floppy

The problem could be with the drive or the disk itself. Try other floppies to see if they make the same sound. If they do, but the drive is working, live with it, like snoring. Your disks won't be harmed.

If the noise problem is with a particular floppy, copy the files off that disk as soon as possible and trash it.

Chapter Eight

Coping with the CD-ROM Drive

CD Doesn't Show Up When You Put It In/Can't Read CD

1. First, make sure that the CD-ROM is inserted correctly. You may be trying to put it in upside down. CD-ROMs are like music CDs, with the data on one side and the label on the other. The label side faces up so you can see the name of the software you're putting in.

2. If you're inserting it correctly and are still having problems, try a different CD-ROM. If the drive doesn't work with any CDs and you haven't recently messed with your CD-ROM drive, you most likely have a software problem.

3. Reinstall your CD-ROM software. If you can't find that software, it's probably part of your operating system. Do a simple reinstallation of the operating system (see "Simple Reinstallation" on page 211).

Audio CD Doesn't Play

To test the audio, you'll need headphones equipped with a one-eighth-inch jack (the kind you use to play a small radio). Most CD-ROM drives have a small jack and volume-control button on the front—if you can't find it there, try the back. If you still can't find it, check your manual. Plug the headphones into the CD-ROM drive. Insert an audio CD into the drive. Most CD-ROM drives should automatically start playing an audio CD once you insert it.

If you can hear the music, you know that your drive is playing the audio. There are two probable reasons, then, why you can't hear it out of your main speakers.

- You may need to turn up the volume control. Check the Sound control panel in Control Panel.
- You may not have a CD audio cable. This is a cable that runs from the back of the CD-ROM drive to the sound device, either a speaker or a sound card. See the manufacturer or your computer manual for information about where to hook this up.

Computer Freezes When CD-ROM Is in Use

While it's locked up, restart the computer. As it's restarting, eject the CD-ROM from the drive. Once started up, try another CD in the computer—preferably an audio CD—to see if the computer will play music, because this will allow you to test the mechanics of the drive without relying on the software. If it plays the audio, you know that the drive operates physically. If not, see chapter 25, "Getting the Best Service." Tell the technician that you suspect a software conflict.

Before taking your CD-ROM drive in for service, spend a few dollars on a CD-ROM cleaning kit. You don't have to bother cleaning CD-ROMs regularly, but there may be a tiny dustball lodged somewhere that's causing the problem on a particular CD-ROM. The little brush that comes with the kit just might dislodge it.

Chapter Nine

Terrors of the Tape Drive

Installation Trouble

If you haven't yet installed a tape drive, take this as a sign: maybe you shouldn't. Tape drives are very temperamental, and problems at the installation stage are like a bad first date—do you really want to stick around for more? The only real advantage to a tape system is that it can handle a large amount of data. If you're considering a tape system, calculate the total amount of your personal files by taking the total amount of information on your computer and subtracting the size of the operating systems and applications. What's left is probably not huge. At the Geek Squad, we find that a removable drive is adequate for most users.

Besides, isn't your major concern recovery, not backup? Since all tape-drive systems use their own unique format, you may have trouble somewhere down the road retrieving your information. (See "Backup Basics" on page 53.)

That said, problems installing a tape drive are always due to hardware/software conflict. Since you are installing the backup system to avoid doom in the event of a crash, and since the number of installation problems you may encounter are too numerous to cover here, we recommend that you hire a professional to do the job.

Problems Restoring Data

If you have this problem, you didn't heed our previous warning about tape backup systems or our cautionary advice came too late. But now that you're in this quandary, first verify that there is data on the tape by using the tape software to call up a listing. (Each tape system gives you a different way to do this.) Do you get either a file or a catalog listing? If you do, but you can't read anything, your best bet is to go straight to a professional tech support firm to try to get your data recovered. You will probably have to pay between $500 and $1,000—yeah, as much as a new computer. If you get no reading at all, chances are your data isn't recoverable, but call a professional firm for an opinion just to be sure.

Freezes

Locking up at any stage is a sign that another piece of hardware—a device such as a CD-ROM or modem—is conflicting with your tape drive. If you've just purchased the tape drive, you are probably eligible for free phone support, and we suggest that you use it. If they can't help you, return the drive and get a removable one.

Some tape-backup problems can be attributed to the software. If you have upgraded to a newer operating system, contact the manufacturer of the tape software to make sure that you have the latest version compatible with the new operating system. If you are already using the latest version of tape software and having problems, your tape drive should be upgraded because it isn't compatible with the new software.

Chapter Ten

Reasoning with the Removable Storage Device

Problems with removable drives like Zip, Jaz, or SuperDisk can almost always be attributed to the nature of the disks. Like floppies, they can go bad when exposed to air, temperature change, dust, and liquids. But on the bright side, even if you do have a problem, you can usually retrieve your data.

Drive Not Working

Mac users: If you are having any kind of trouble, the best place to start is reinstalling the software.

Windows 95/98 users: Go to Control Panel | System | Device Manager | Ports. If the LPT or printer port is not listed, or it is listed and you see a yellow exclamation point, contact your computer manufacturer.

Can't Read Disk

1. To test the drive, insert a disk that you know is OK. If the drive isn't reading any disks, reinstall the software that came with it (see "Resolving Driver/Extension Conflicts–Reinstalling Drivers/Extensions" on page 213). If that doesn't work, go to step 2.
2. Test the disk. If you're using a diskette from a common removable-drive system like a Zip drive, try it in another computer. If you can access the files, there's something wrong with your drive.
3. Test the disk on another drive. If you don't happen to have an extra drive sitting around, check the Yellow Pages under "Graphic Services Suppliers." These are typesetting services, or what used to be called printers, and they have an endless variety of removable drives because who knows what kind of material their clients might walk in with. They're almost guaranteed to have one like yours. Use your social skills to see if someone will take your disk into the back office and give it a quick test. (If they invite *you* into the back office with them, use your judgment.)

Graphic-services suppliers are brainy types who are often more helpful than your corner computer store.

REASONING
WITH THE
REMOVABLE
STORAGE
DEVICE
105

Disk Noisy When Inserted

Chomp. Chomp. Burp. Burp. It's not Jurassic Park, but it's a problem. It's either the drive or the disk. Narrow down the possibilities by eliminating what it isn't.

1. Try another disk. If it stays calm and silent, the first one you tried is bad news. Copy the files if you can and trash it.
2. If any disk produces a noise that we know as the dreaded "click of death," your equipment is defective. Eject the disk; stay as far away from the drive as you can. Contact the manufacturer or whoever sold you the drive and get a replacement.

Computer Freezes When Drive Is Used

If you have installed a removable-drive system that uses the external parallel port that's shared with the printer, and the printer and/or drive has or causes a problem such as freezing, talk to the printer manufacturer, not the driver manufacturer.

Can't Write to Disk/Error Message Appears

1. Eject the disk and see if it is locked.
2. Try another disk.
3. Check the format. Is it formatted? Is it properly formatted for Mac or Windows? Contact the drive manufacturer for help.

Chapter Eleven

Calming the Keyboard

Computer keyboards and electronic keyboards are two different animals. For example, while "jamming" on an electronic keyboard is encouraged and possibly fruitful, "jamming" on a computer keyboard will likely produce nothing but further jamming—your keys might stick together.

Once you have gotten the PC keyboard turned on, ending the relationship may be a problem (a concept you may have also experienced in your social life). Do not plug or unplug the keyboard unless the computer is off. Macs don't seem to care whether you do this, and some of the newer PCs can be forgiving, but the older ones get very cranky. Still, if you unplug and then replug, you not only lose the data in the document you're working in, but you may actually corrupt the hard drive by turning off power in the middle of a program.

Here's a little mantra to repeat to yourself about keyboards: they rarely break. If you have a problem with the "keyboard," you're probably really having a problem with the connection to the keyboard. It's even possible that you have a virus. On the other hand, if you've got two keys that don't work, especially if they're near each other and if you've recently spilled something, this probably is a keyboard problem.

Keyboards are relatively inexpensive. You may be able to get a used keyboard for as little as $20. So, don't sweat the small stuff. If you have in fact got a keyboard problem, it makes more sense to replace it than to spend much time (or any money) on repair. Nevertheless, some easy rescues are worth a try.

Spill on Keyboard

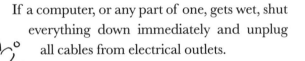

If a computer, or any part of one, gets wet, shut everything down immediately and unplug all cables from electrical outlets.

• If you spilled water and cut the power right away, you'll be OK. Water will normally evaporate, but it'll take a while, depending on how much water was spilled—"a while" could be two to three days. To speed up the process, you will need a hair dryer. (You will not need a brush.) Set the dryer to medium and wave it back and forth over the keyboard, holding it six to ten inches away. Purse your lips and murmur "Perfect, perfect." (OK, we're kidding about the murmuring.) Don't get too close to the keyboard: you will not burn its hair, but you could melt the plastic.
• Coffee or soda spills are a little more serious. Oils and sugars in

these items can gunk up moving parts in a keyboard as well as the human body. *If there is a spill, abort all keyboard operations immediately. Any attempt to operate a keyboard in this situation will cause further damage.* Take the computer to a repair shop for a cleaning as quickly as possible, or the damage might be irreparable. If you have to keep working and can't wait for a repair, buy another keyboard. That will cost you a lot less than replacing the entire computer.

• As a technique of last resort, try what we call the McGyver rescue: Place the keyboard facedown in the dishwasher. Coil the cord and tie it with a twist-tie so that it won't drop down and get caught in the motor. Do not add soap, and run the dishwasher. Make sure that it's set to "air dry" or a similar setting and not to "heat dry." Once the dishwasher is done and you remove the keyboard, wait another eight hours before putting it back into service.

Sparkling clean work space

BALLOONING INTO A HERD OF GAZELLES IN NAIROBI

It's raining out so
naturally
I asked the young ladies
waiting on the counter
at the Mac store
if I could double-wrap
my new keyboard
in two plastic bags
plus
a third shopping bag
because, as
I explained,
that's why I'm here to begin with
—the spill, you know—
so there's no sense in
getting the
new one wet.
At the store
they exclaimed
You really
spilled
ginger ale
on your keyboard?
You really did it?
Yes, I say quite modestly,
with the same tone
and self-effacement
I use
when
acknowledging
my experiences
drinking from the Ganges,
leading the way on the primitive trail
in Arches National Park
and
ballooning into a herd of gazelles
in
Nairobi.
I did it
and lived to tell
the tale.

—*Martha Rose Reeves*

Windows: Keyboard Not Working

1. If the Num Lock and Cap Lock keys don't light up, go to step 4.
2. If the Num Lock and Cap Lock keys light up, but the keyboard isn't working, turn off the computer and restart with minimum system startup. When it says "Starting Windows95" or "Starting Windows98," hit F8. From the menu that appears, choose Safe Mode. Try to type again.
3. If the keyboard still doesn't work, turn off the machine and try to boot from an emergency boot disk (see "EMS for a Crashed Computer" on page 62).

    Windows users: When the emergency boot disk comes up, you will see the letter A followed by a colon (:) on the screen. To know if your hard drive is working, type in a C followed by a colon and then hit Enter. Now if you type "DIR" you will see all the directories that are on the drive.

    • If your keyboard operates from an emergency boot disk, but still won't start up when you boot normally, see chapter 25, "Getting the Best Service."
    • If the keyboard won't operate when you use an emergency boot disk, you might need a new keyboard. Before you buy, however, have someone at the store test your present keyboard. This service takes no more than a minute or two, and you shouldn't be charged for it (if they try to charge you, go to another store). If your keyboard is on its best behavior with the salesperson, your problem may be with the port. So go starboard. (Just kidding.) See chapter 25, "Getting the Best Service."

4. If the Num Lock and Cap Lock keys do not light up when you turn on the computer, turn it off. Unplug the keyboard and check the pins in the cable.

    • If pins are bent, don't try to straighten them out, as they may break off. Since the cable is attached to the keyboard, you will need a new keyboard.
    • If pins are not bent, replug the cable, making sure you've got a snug fit.

5. If the Num Lock and Cap Lock keys still don't light, replace the keyboard.

Once you get to the store, tell the technician everything you've done so far. This is not to elicit sympathy, but to make it easier for him to resolve the problem, which is probably a software conflict.

Mac: Keyboard Not Working

• If the keyboard seems to be in cardiac arrest but your mouse is still perky, use minimum system startup. Turn off the computer, then hold down the Shift key the minute you turn it back on. Click System | Control Panel. Look for a file called Easy Access. Drag this file to the trash can. Then go under the Special menu and click Restart.

We solve this problem so easily and so frequently—we'd say it comes up at least once a day—that it's helped build our reputation as geniuses, so it's almost painful to just give it away like this. (Did Houdini reveal his tricks?) But OK. Here's the story: Easy Access is a special piece of software designed for the handicapped. It allows them to reprogram the buttons on the keyboard depending on their specific handicap. People very often activate it inadvertently and their keyboard stops responding. If you don't need this software, trashing it will usually solve the problem of the keyboard not responding.

• If the Num Lock and Cap Lock keys do not light up when you turn on the computer, consult the section that precedes this one for what to do. However, if the pins in your cable are bent, since the cable is detachable, you can simply get a new cable.

One Key Doesn't Work

• If an external keyboard works perfectly except for a single key that has turned into the black sheep of the family, it's probably just a little dirty. Try to remove it. Most keys can be lifted off the rubber or spring mecha-

nism underneath. Gently pry up the key cover using a butter knife or other similarly unthreatening tool. Use a can of compressed air or blow into the key to clear out any tiny dust balls, and then blow into the space in the keyboard to do the same. Press down gently on the space where the plastic key was to test for buoyancy. If everything looks dandy, replace the key cover.

• If a key is sticking, the problem may be dust or a sticky liquid that has been spilled.

Turn off the computer. (If you need to get work done right away, use another keyboard. If fixing the key requires cleaning the keyboard, you may have a long wait before you can put it back in operation.) Gently pull off the problem key and clean the area with compressed air or a lint-free cloth. Hint: Clean cloth diapers are lint-free. So are most kitchen towels. Terry cloth towels are not.

If you've had a spill, you may need to use a conventional cleaning liquid such as Windex. Caution: Wait eight hours to make sure your computer is thoroughly dry before you turn it back on.

If all else fails, try the McGyver technique described at the beginning of the chapter.

• If you've tried everything and the key still sticks, use another keyboard.

If that works perfectly, you know you have a keyboard problem. Repair or replace the keyboard.

If it doesn't work perfectly, you might have a virus. Or maybe it's user error. Or maybe it's just one of those little guys in the computer taking a half hour off. Turn the machine off, go have a cup of coffee, take a break, then turn it on again. If you're still having problems, see chapter 25, "Getting the Best Service."

Pressing One Key Delivers Another Character

A common laptop problem. You type "ship," and the machine writes "shin" . . . or worse. The cable that connects the keyboard to the rest of the laptop has become loose and is crossing signals.

Typically, we tell this to a customer and they express astonishment. How did the cable get loose? So we ask, "Had your RAM upgraded at an electronics store recently?" And yes, they have. Someone who serviced the computer didn't put it back together right. Or else, this is just one of those things that happens. People fail to remember there is no stasis in the universe. When you put a cable into place, it's pinched between two pieces of metal bent toward each other. Over time, you get the wiggle effect. The thing works itself out of place. Long story short, you need a technician. See chapter 25, "Getting the Best Service."

Before you get talked into buying a new keyboard, explain to the repair technician that you think the problem is a loose cable.

Chapter Twelve

Taming the Mouse/ Pointer Device

Every day we Geeks are reminded that what is ridiculously obvious to us may be a Sphinxian mystery to someone else. One customer, for example, couldn't find a reliable mouse. She tried several and not a one worked. But when she dropped off the questionable equipment, we could find nothing wrong with the software, the computer, or any of the mice. Then one of our resourceful technicians asked her to demonstrate her mousing technique. Bingo. She held the mouse in the air, pointed it at the computer and clicked away. You, of course, know better.

Mouse Needs CPR

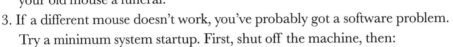

1. If it appears that your mouse has swallowed some poisoned cheese and is dead on its pad, shut down the computer. Disconnect it from the rear of the computer and try reconnecting it firmly.
2. If that doesn't work, try a new mouse. If it works, give your old mouse a funeral.
3. If a different mouse doesn't work, you've probably got a software problem. Try a minimum system startup. First, shut off the machine, then:

   Mac users: Hold down the Shift key the minute you turn the computer on.
   • If that doesn't work, reinstall your system software, using the disk that came with your computer.
   • If the minimum system startup does make the mouse work, you have a software issue. See "Resolving Driver/Extension Conflicts–Reinstalling Drivers/Extensions" on page 213.

   Windows users: Hit F8 when computer says "Starting Windows95." A menu will appear. Choose Safe Mode.
   • If this allows you to use your mouse, turn off the machine. Restart and use the diskette that came with your mouse to reinstall it. (Safe Mode is only a temporary fix.)
   • If the mouse doesn't work, reinstall your system software.

4. If none of this works and you haven't changed anything recently—such as installed an external modem—you have a hardware problem. See chapter 25, "Getting the Best Service."
5. If you've recently installed an external modem, and you have a second serial port, try connecting the modem to that.
6. If that fails, connect a different mouse to your computer.
   • If it works, replace your mouse.
   • If a new mouse fails, see chapter 25, "Getting the Best Service."

Windows: Mouse Won't Cooperate with Modem

This is a common problem because the mouse and an internal modem sometimes share the same communication port, and they just don't get along. If you have a second port for your mouse, try it. If that doesn't work, see chapter 25, "Getting the Best Service."

Mouse Lies Down on the Job

If your mouse is working fitfully, remember that it's like your car: it runs better when it's clean. To clean it, turn it over and find the circular ring. Think of it as the mouse belly button. Unscrew it. When you look inside, you will no doubt discover that a mouse is an indiscriminate eater and its intestines are a mess. Clean them out. Do not use a cotton swab, because it will leave little tiny hairs. Instead, get a poking tool, or tweezers, that can scrape and pull out the dirt. Replace the ring. Now your mouse should drive like a Lexus.

Did you know that you can mickey with the mouse? Options include adjusting the speed and adjusting the tracer to increase the size of the arrow pointer, which may make tracking easier for you.

Mac users: Select Apple | Control Panel | Mouse.

Windows 95/98 users: Select Settings | Control Panel | Mouse.

Now we'll tell you something about trackballs that most people don't yet know. Trackballs are exactly the same size as billiard balls because they *are* billiard balls. The computer equipment folks realized that it was cheaper to buy these balls, unfinished, than to manufacture new and different-size balls. To liven up your trackball setup, replace the ball with an eight ball (or other ball of your choice).

Chapter Thirteen

Scanner Solutions

Scanning for Beginners

Scanning an image such as a photograph or a document so that it's in your computer is a nifty trick. If there are pages of text you have to incorporate into something that's already in your computer, don't retype: head to a computer service center. They'll charge you something like $10 to scan the first page, $2 for subsequent pages. Or buy a scanner yourself. They're less than $100.

Originally, scanners could scan only pictures. Now that they've grown up a little, they've learned to read, thanks to OCR (optical character recognition) software, which converts a scanned image of text into a text file by "looking" at the image and differentiating between, say, an "M" and a "W."

Many scanners come with free scanning and OCR software. Omnipage, by Caere, Inc., is very high-quality software.

Mac users: With its modems, Global Village ships a great software package called Global Fax OCR. With it, as you view faxes received, you can use the Save As command to automatically convert a fax into the text of your choice. There are always a few little glitches in terms of formatting—you may not get text in bold or underlined—but the accuracy is 90 to 95 percent.

If you need help in scanning, the experts, hands-down, are graphic-service bureaus, newspeak for printers, who have learned to scan all kinds of art and text to make a printable page. (Check the Yellow Pages under "Graphic Services.")

Scanning Without a Scanner

If you have a modem, you probably have the capacity to send and receive faxes. You can equip the modem with special OCR software that converts a scanned image of text into a text file. See "Sending/Receiving a Computer File Using a Fax" on page 202.

If there's an item that you want scanned, but you have no scanner or your scanner is broken, fax the item to your computer modem. Save it as an image and work on it with editing software.

SIBLING RIVALRY

These things are never planned for.
Somehow you just wake up
throwing up and you
know
deep inside your heart it
wasn't bad tuna fish.
I loaded Brainiac!
and the installation
was successful.
I went to open it and
Bingo!
The message:
You need a Power Mac to run this
program.
I immediately turned up
the volume on the CD player on my Performa
and tried to open Brainiac! one more time
to no avail.
Alas:
the thing I had done without . . .
the thing I did not need . . .
the thing I would now
definitely be out to get:
A Powerbook
(while knowing I would never let my present
hardworking Performa go).
La-la-la sang my
CD-ROM.
Was my Mac noticing?
I could only
hope not.
Later, the next evening

actually,
in I walked.
Powerbook in hand.
Brainiac! already loaded
and tested.
Do I introduce them?
Do I take it to another room
and pretend it doesn't exist?
Soon my high shrill
falsetto tones will
no longer fool my Performa.
He'll guess for sure.
Where are you taking the scanner?
he'll ask.
How do I tell the one who has tirelessly scanned countless
family photographs
that it can't handle
optical character recognition?
How do you ask
a Mac you love
if it would mind very much if
you borrow its earphone set
just for a minute
to listen to audio
over the Net.
I know I'll be celebrating the
new one's birthday
during the night for the
next few years.
All this comes from
spoiling the first-born.

—*Martha Rose Reeves*

Scanner Doesn't Scan

1. If your scanner seems to be on the blink, don't take it for servicing until you reinstall the driver (see "Resolving Driver/Extension Conflicts–Reinstalling Drivers/Extensions" on page 213) and perform a test scan.
2. If the test fails, check the connections between the computer and the scanner. *Shhh*—listen quietly. If you hear movement inside the scanner but it is still not working, our guess is that the problem is with your computer. If the scanner is silent, then the problem is with the scanner.
3. Attach the scanner to another machine and see if it's willing to play with a different partner. If it's still unconscious, replace it. Since you can get one for under $100, repairing a scanner is generally not worth the cost.
4. The most likely scenario is that you have a software problem. You may be trying to get an old scanner to work with a new computer. The usual solution—reinstalling the driver—might not do the trick, because a reinstallation of scanner software doesn't always override the driver that's already there. But if you try to take the old driver out, it may take your video driver with it. Call the manufacturer for help.

When you call for tech support, they'll probably tell you to send the scanner in for repair. It will be helpful if you can tell them that you've tested the scanner and it already works, but you need someone who can help walk you through the setup to check for software problems. You won't waste time and money packing up and sending off a machine that's mechanically perfect, and once the guy on the other end realizes you've already jumped through some of the hoops, he'll probably be a little more willing to help you work things out on the phone.

Scanner Light Isn't Working

Inside each scanner is a fluorescent bulb approximately eight inches long that lasts around three to five years. If your scanner is about to celebrate a birthday and is otherwise working normally, most likely the bulb has burned out. See chapter 25, "Getting the Best Service."

 When you take the scanner in, tell the repair technician that you suspect you need a new bulb.

How many technicians does it take to change a scanner light bulb? Two. One to change the bulb and the other to calm down the customer who has just found out that a new scanner bulb costs about $200.

Chapter Fourteen

Pointers for Printers

Printer Having a Tantrum

Everything's stuck. Nothing's working right. Give your printer the equivalent of "If you don't start behaving right now, I'm sending you to your room for a time-out"—turn off the printer, then turn off the computer. Wait ten seconds. Turn on the printer, then turn on the computer. You'd be amazed at how often this works.

Not Printing

Here we are again, trying to impress upon you the importance of thinking in a logical sequence. To pinpoint what's wrong with your printer (or computer), go through the following steps:

1. **Is it a power problem?** Shut the computer off, then turn the printer off. Is the printer plugged in? Then check that the cable is plugged into both the computer and the printer. Finally, turn both items back on. Did the computer go on and not the printer? The printer needs servicing.

2. **Is it a document problem?** Try to print a document other than the one that's giving you trouble. If you can, you know something is wrong with the original document. The program or computer somehow corrupted it. If you need the data in the nonprinting document, try this: Open a new document in the same program. Cut and paste the text from the bad document to this new, blank window and then try to print from the new window. If that works, trash the old document. If it doesn't, try to save the original document in a different format. Choose Save As, and select Text Only or Basic Text, then see if you can print that.

3. **Is it an application problem?** If you can't print any other documents from the application you're working on (Microsoft Word, for example), try printing something from another application. If that works, then your problem is with your application software. See "Can't Print from Application" on page 161.

4. **Is it a mechanical problem?** If you have trouble printing from two or more programs, this may be the case. To see if the printer is functioning mechanically, print a test page. Each printer has its own way of performing the equivalent of its own electrocardiogram. It usually involves turning the printer off and then turning it back on while holding down a particular combination of buttons. Check the manual for specific instructions, or call the manufacturer for tech support. If the printer does not print a test page, there is something mechanically wrong with it. See chapter 25, "Getting the Best Service."

5. **Is it a problem with the software from your printer?** If the printer does print a test page but you can't print from your computer, you need to reinstall your printer driver and printer software. Here's how:

   Mac users: If the printer appears on your desktop, drag it to the trash before doing a reinstallation. (If the printer's in your Chooser, don't bother. The reinstallation will automatically overwrite what's already there.)

Windows users: Look under Start | Settings | Printer. Click on your old printer and hit the Delete key on your keyboard.

If you don't have a copy of your printer software, you can download it from the Internet. The manufacturer is happy to provide it this way. Why not? The software is useless if you don't own a printer. And supplying the software via the Net saves the manufacturer from annoying calls from people like you. Or try an Action Jackson maneuver and offer $20 to a kid from the computer store to put a copy on a disk for you.

6. **Is it the cable?** Once the reinstallation is done, if you still can't print, try replacing the printer cable. Bring the one you're using to the computer store, have them test it, and, if it's faulty, buy a new one (about $10).
7. **If you're still having problems,** it's time to face the music. Your printer needs repair. Don't go to a computer-repair center—a lot of them, including the Geek Squad, don't even fix printers. Instead, look in the Yellow Pages for a place that repairs copiers. Printers and copiers are mechanically very similar.

Produces Blank Page

If the printer seems to be printing but produces only a blank page, the solution is to get into your car and drive to an office-supply shop. You probably just need a new toner or ink cartridge. Make sure you know the model number, or bring the old one for reference. Your printer manual will give you instructions on installing a new one. There might even be a pictogram inside the printer or on the cartridge to show you how. It's easy. (What's hard is remembering to always keep a spare on hand for just this sort of emergency.)

Prints Garbage

1. If your printer appears to be printing secret coded messages from space, do not alert the authorities. No one will believe you (remember Roswell) and, besides, you can clear up the problem by simply reinstalling the printer software from the original disks or CD-ROM. See item 5 under "Not Printing" on page 125.

2. If the aliens still seem to be attempting to communicate, the problem may be the printer cable. A bad one can cause crossed signals that create this problem. Bring your cable to the computer store, have them test it, and, if it's faulty, buy a new one (about $10).

Do you have a switchbox on your computer that connects two printers to one part? That may be the problem. Even if you've set everything up 100 percent perfectly, some printers just don't play well with others. Replace the printer, or see if you can get updated printer software that will get things playing together nicely.

Windows 95 users: First, check to see if you're using Windows 95 Revision B. Go to the Start menu and to Settings | Control Panel | System Control Panel. It will list your version of Windows and will say 4.00.95. If those numbers are not followed by any letter, go to the Microsoft Web site (www.microsoft.com) and locate the file called Service Pack 1 for Windows 95. Download that and install it. That may solve your problem.

3. Try another application to see if the print quality from it is problematic as well. If it is, you may need to reinstall the printer software, or your printer software may be corrupt. See chapter 25, "Getting the Best Service."
4. If weirdness happens only on a single document, copy the material, paste it into a new file, and print from the new one. Or change the layout of the troublesome area—for example, add to or subtract from a particular paragraph—and your problem may be solved. Sometimes those little guys inside the computer like to play jokes.
5. If all else fails, take machine to a place that repairs copiers to see if they can find and correct a mechanical problem.

Paper Jam

1. Paper jam has no calories but has no taste, either, so no one likes it. It may be caused by too little or too much paper in the paper tray. Like Goldilocks, the printer wants the amount to be just right.

2. A small bit of paper caught in the printer can cause a jam. Remove all paper from the paper tray. Pop the printer cover, remove the toner and/or ink cartridge, and clean out any confettilike pieces. Be gentle. Aggressive pulling may cause more stray bits and a worse jam.

CAUTION: When removing paper from the path, pull it out gently from the rear, never from the front.

3. If the printer is still eating paper, take it to the doc. Find one at a copier-repair center (not a computer-repair center).

Won't Grab Paper

If you hear the machine grinding away but it doesn't grab paper, check to see whether you have inadvertently pushed a lever on the printer that changes the setting from grabbing paper to grabbing envelopes.

Won't Print from One Particular Program

Windows users: If you are running a DOS program, your problem is probably that you have an old program running under DOS mode within Windows. The drivers are different from the regular Windows driver, so even if the printer is set up and working perfectly under other programs, it may not work with this one. Look at the program's manuals for instructions about setting up the printer. More than likely, the printer described will not be exactly the same as the one you have because the DOS manual is old, so look for printers that are in the same family—same brand or same type, such as inkjet or laser.

ON FILLING THE PAPER BIN ON YOUR PRINTER

Do you suppose it makes
no sense
when filling
the paper bin
on your printer
to caress its front panel
just a bit
like the side flank
of an eager
golden retriever
as
if
the
paper
were
its favorite brand of
canned dog food?

—Martha Rose Reeves

Quality Is Poor

1. If the print is too dark or too light, or the color is poor, changing the print-density setting that controls darkness or lightness might be the solution. If there is no Print Density option showing in the Print window, you may find it if you click Options | Settings.

   If you have a laser printer and blacks are too intense or too light, change the setting of the printer density wheel. (Check the manual that came with your printer.)

2. If image remains too light, or blacks occasionally print gray, and, especially, if you have blotches, before you shell out for a new toner cartridge, first empty and then reload the paper tray, to make sure the paper goes through smoothly. Then deal with toner cartridge. The internal heat of the printer causes toner particles to clump together like teenagers at a mixer. Unclump them and you can extend the life of your cartridge by as much as 30 percent. To do this, first press the small button on the top or the side of the printer to open the cover. Pull the cartridge out, hold it horizontally, and shake it from side to side. A diagram illustrating this technique is in your printer manual (right next to the instructions on how to do the funky chicken). Reinstall and voilà! Problem's solved. But if the clumping problem is persistent, get a can of compressed air and squeeze a shot into the toner cartridge.

3. If you have an inkjet printer, remember that the operative word is "ink." Ink is dirty, and dirty is bad. Rule #1: Give the ink cartridge a cleaning once a week, or every thirty pages or so. Every inkjet printer has a function in the printer-utility software that will do the cleaning for you, just like a housekeeper.

   If a cleaning doesn't help, replace the ink cartridge.

Can't Find Supplies for Printer

- A laser printer–repair company can recharge a laser printer toner cartridge for you.
- Computer and office-supply stores sell inkjet refill kits. These come with a syringe and a vial of ink that you can inject into an opening on the top of your ink cartridge. Afterward, you can use the syringe to play doctor.
- If you're still hanging on to a dot matrix printer and can't find a replacement ribbon, here's a tip that an eccentric like you will love: A ribbon fades because the ink particles begin to dry out, but it still has a lot of ink left in it. A lubricant such as WD-40 can loosen and refresh it.

1. Spread out some newspaper on a table. When you've finished rereading the articles you missed the first time around, continue to step 2.
2. Gently pull the ribbon out of the cartridge onto the newspaper, taking care not to tangle it.
3. Flatten out the ribbon.
4. Holding a can of WD-40 about twelve to fifteen inches away, spray a gentle mist on the ribbon.
5. Wait thirty minutes for the mist to dry.
6. Recoil the ribbon in its case, and reinstall it in the printer.

Print a few test pages. You should see an improved print quality. (Let us know if you come up with any suggestions on how to recycle your empty WD-40 can.)

Mac: Printer Quits Partway Through Job

We don't promise high-quality type and graphics, but if you want to get a hard copy of what's on your screen, and your printer suddenly decides to try a work stoppage, this is worth a try. When the document is on your screen, press Command+Shift+3. You'll hear a "click," as if you were taking a snapshot. In fact, you're taking a "picture" of whatever is in the window. Scroll down until you've got a window full of new copy, then press

Command+Shift+3 again. Each snapshot is saved on your hard drive as a PICT file (named Picture 1, Picture 2, Picture 3, and so on). Look under Find File and locate TeachText or SimpleText. Click to open one or the other and you will find the PICT files, which can be opened and printed.

Printing Sideways

If you want a horizontal image on the paper, look under the File menu and choose Page Setup. Click the correct icon to change the layout from portrait (up and down) to landscape (sideways).

Printing Envelopes

Many new word-processing programs contain templates for envelopes. Consult your program's manual. If you don't have a template, here's how to make one:

Under File, choose Page Setup. Paper type is probably set at "letter." Change that to #10 envelope, or com 10 (depending on the options listed). You may also have to change the printing orientation from portrait (up and down) to landscape (sideways—see "Printing Sideways," above.)

Type an address on the screen, then print your results onto regular 8½-x-11 paper and see if it looks right. Then work with an envelope. An icon on your printer may indicate how to insert the envelope; if not, refer to your manual. The printer may also have a lever that changes position in order to grab an envelope rather than a sheet of paper.

You may have to play around with the margin settings to get the placement of the address and the return address exactly as you want it. Once you have it, save it as a file called "Personal Envelope." Now you've got a template. Get rid of your typewriter. But don't throw out your pen.

Chapter Fifteen
Making the Modem
Mind You

Modem Not Working

Modems are durable devices that rarely break. So, any problem you have will probably be along the lines of a "modems are from Mars, computers are from Mercury" kind of thing. The modem is working, but when it talks to your software program (such as America Online or a browser), the software program doesn't hear, or mishears, it.

Here is a quick test to determine whether your modem problem is hardware- or software-related:

Mac users:

1. First, make sure that any fax or caller ID software is disabled. (Quit those programs.)
2. Open your terminal program, which is a piece of software that allows you to talk to the modem. It will test to see whether the modem is physically operating. Global Village comes with a program called Zterm. Most other manufacturers use Mac CommCenter. Search for either of those words on your hard drive.
3. In the blank terminal window, you'll see a blinking cursor. Type "AT." Press the Enter or Return key.
4. If you see an "OK" appear on the screen, at least you know that your modem is functioning properly, though it might not be working right with every program.
5. If you did NOT see an "OK," plug your modem into a different port. (Modems on a Mac can be plugged into either the printer or modem port, and sometimes one of them goes bad.) Set the software to look for the modem on that port by holding down Shift as Zterm starts. Then start with step 2. If you still don't get an OK, your modem is having a physical problem. Contact the manufacturer and report what you have already tried.

Windows 3.X users:

1. Under the Accessories program group, choose Terminal.
2. In the blank terminal window, you'll see a blinking cursor. Type "AT." Press the Return or Enter key.
3. If you see an "OK" appear on the screen, you know that your modem is working properly, though you may still be having problems.
4. If you did NOT see an "OK" after typing the AT command, try a different COM port. For each program, how to set the COM port is different.
5. Under the Settings menu, you will find a setting for COM1 through COM4.
6. Try COM1, then click OK.
7. Return to the blank terminal window, and try the "AT" command again (step 2).
8. Repeat until you have gotten an "OK" or tried each of the four COM ports.

If you still cannot get the computer to give you an OK after typing AT in the terminal window for each COM port, you have a hardware problem. If the modem is OK, there could be an improper configuration of the physical connection settings, or a setting on the modem itself. Call the modem's tech-support line and tell them which tests you have already run.

Windows 95/98 users:
1. Start | Settings | Control Panel | Modems Control Panel.
2. See if your modem is listed. Remove other modems by clicking on them, then clicking the Remove button in the window.
3. Go to Diagnostics tab and click Modem | More Info. A window should pop up with information about your modem. If it doesn't, leave the Modem control panel and go to System control panel and open the Device Manager tab. Click Modem | Properties. If it reports conflicts, it will prompt you what to do.

Seems Slow

Noise (strange interference) on the line can slow down the modem. Ask the phone company to test the line. If after they check the line from the main office you still think you have line problems, ask that the phone company make a house call to test everything.

Slow modem? Call your provider

More likely than a problem with the phone line is a problem with your service provider or your modem. Contact your service provider (America Online, your ISP, whatever) to report your problem and get them to walk you through a solution. If that fails, it's the modem that isn't working.

Particular Program Can't See the Modem

Even if only one program works, you know that your modem is OK. So try to point the finger of blame in another direction by attempting the following:

1. Verify that the settings are right, following instructions in "Modem Not Working" on page 135. (Wrong settings are usually the problem.)
2. Check that the telephone line plugged into the modem is working. Unplug the connection from the back of the computer and plug it into a regular phone, using the same cable, and see if the line is good.
3. Quit all other applications that use your modem (such as a fax) while using the program that you want to use.
4. If problem persists, reinstall the program.

Dialing Problems

With Home Phone

If there's no dial tone, or the modem won't dial, check that the phone is working. (*Duh.*) Maybe you left another phone off the hook somewhere. Maybe the phone line is down. Maybe you didn't pay your phone bill.

With Office Phone

CAUTION: If you're at work, check with your office administrator before you attempt to connect your modem to the company system. Most won't allow it, and if you try it, you may damage your modem.

With some systems, you have to first dial an outside line. After you type the 9 or 8 (whichever the system requires), type a comma before the phone number. (The comma inserts a half-second pause.)

As a last resort, try plugging another computer into that same phone line in the same location to test it. Sometimes a modem's on/off hook switch will go bad and you'll get an erroneous "No Dial Tone" message. If you hear the modem click, but it reports "No Dial Tone," try connecting from a different computer. If it works, the problem is with the first computer. Or with your phone line.

Disabling Call Waiting

Call waiting may interrupt a download or file transfer over the modem. If you're planning to download, first temporarily disable call waiting.

Press these four keys: star, seven, zero, comma (*70,) before you dial the number that you'll be connecting to. (The comma is a half-second pause.) When you hang up, call waiting will kick back in.

Knowing how to disable call waiting is a very useful trick. Try it when you are about to make an important business call or get into a serious phone session with a Significant Other and don't want to be interrupted by someone trying to sell you a magazine.

 Radio Shack sells a device called a Teleprotector (less than $10) that you can put on an extension phone to keep your connection from being broken if someone picks up the phone while you're telecommunicating.

Silent Modem

The sound of silence may be ominous. Check modem settings under the Modem control panel or in your software. Both should be set to "On."

Some people prefer to leave the sound off so they don't have to hear that ear-piercing screech when the modem connects. Other people actually like this sound. These same people also tend to have bug collections.

Connection Failure

Important distinction: when does the modem poop out—before it dials, or after you're connected? If it fails before it dials, go to "Modem Not Working" on page

135. If the modem fails in the middle of dialing, the cause is most likely a conflict between hardware and software:

1. Reinstall your modem software. (See "Resolving Driver/Extension Conflicts–Reinstalling Drivers/Extensions" on page 213.)
2. Try a different phone jack. Sometimes wires get bent or corrupted, and just moving the modem will solve the problem. Even a modem needs a change of scene once in a while.
3. Try a different phone line. Take your modem to the next office or next door. If that works, then your problem is on the line. Call the phone company.
4. Try a different modem. Since repairing the old one may cost $100, you might be better off buying a new one.

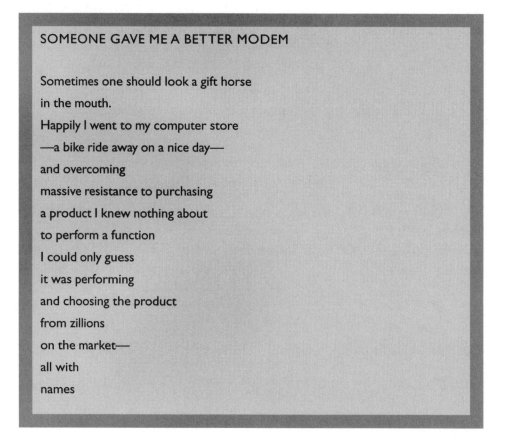

SOMEONE GAVE ME A BETTER MODEM

Sometimes one should look a gift horse

in the mouth.

Happily I went to my computer store

—a bike ride away on a nice day—

and overcoming

massive resistance to purchasing

a product I knew nothing about

to perform a function

I could only guess

it was performing

and choosing the product

from zillions

on the market—

all with

names

which made me

feel

as if

(even without the aid of Zen

and transcendentalism)

I would be able to connect

directly with the

center of the

universe's

thalmus—

I

selected a

modem;

whereupon,

on getting it home

and unloading

it from

my purple pannier

(French for bicycle basket)

I was immediately offered

for free

a faster,

taller,

thinner,

more costly

model

in exchange for mine.

The only

small problem

was that

occasionally

the would-be gift model

without reason

had the occasional habit

of suddenly terminating the telephone connection.

Still,

I grabbed the offer

figuring—

and I guarantee you this was my thinking—

that in my household

reason ruled

and it would have no

justification

for such erratic

behavior.

But its pattern of sudden disconnects

persisted.

Which goes to

show

you

that for modems,

it's heredity

and

not environment

that counts.

—Martha Rose Reeves

Faxing on Your Computer

Did you know that almost every modem also has the capacity to be a fax machine? Once you have installed fax software, anything you can print you can also fax, so every machine in the world can deliver your message without your having to print it out and then fax it. Here's how to get started:

Mac users: Fax capability is not built directly into the operating system, but Global Village, which makes great modems for Macs, also produces some of the best fax software.

Windows 95/98 users: Fax software is automatically included in this program. Press the F1 key for help and search for "faxing."

Windows 3.X users: Purchase fax software such as Symantec.

MANUAL RECEIVE

When I made up my stationery
on my home printer
I listed my name and address,
then my telephone number.
Right underneath,
I made the claim that
it doubled as
my fax number,
stating optimistically
(Manual Only)
meaning, First you call me
and you tell me you want to send a fax
and I say blithely,
Give me five minutes first.
I then dash upstairs to my answering machine,
turning off
the Answer On,

then downstairs to start up
my computer,
then back upstairs
to unplug my answering machine completely
so it won't automatically reset
to Answer On,
And then
I pull down
Manual Receive,
and I am ready to click
Receive Fax,
when my backup answering service—
which will activate
after five rings—
comes to mind.
I try to dial my
special box and type in my special code
and change the
trigger ring delay
to nine
and by now,
Manual Receive
has defaulted
to Auto Receive,
and my West Coast caller
has attempted
in vain
six times
to send me a
fax.
I'm exhausted
and thinking
Frémont may have had
the better idea
by just
moving to California.

—*Martha Rose Reeves*

Chapter Sixteen

Sound-Card Solutions

The sound card is the hardware that makes it possible for you to hear all sounds, from the startup "bong" to an error "beep." On all Macs and some PCs the sound card is built into the motherboard, while on other PCs it goes into a slot. To hear the sound from PCs, you need speakers, for which there are jacks in the rear. Macs have internal speakers, but you can add external speakers so the sound will be louder and in stereo.

If you upgrade a CD-ROM drive, you'll probably need to upgrade your sound card, too. These two have to work as a team. If they don't get along, you're out of luck.

No Sound

First, try the obvious—remove your earmuffs. Then:

1. Is the power supply working? Plug in a lamp or other electrical device to test it.
2. Is your AC power plugged into the speakers? Or should you check the batteries?
3. Are speakers plugged into the speaker port?
4. Try unplugging, then replugging the speakers.
5. Put in an audio CD. If you can hear it playing, you know that the sound works. If it doesn't, most CD-ROM drives have a headphone jack in the front of the computer. Even if the sound card is not working and speakers aren't producing sound, plug headphones into the front of the CD drive.
6. If you hear sound through the headphones, check the volume in the computer settings. (If you don't, skip the following and go to step 7.)

   Mac users: Go to Control Panel | Sound (or, in operating systems 7.6 and above, Control Panel | Monitors and Sound) and make sure that the volume is turned up.

   Windows 3.X users: If the sound card has volume control, make sure that it's turned up.

   Windows 95/98 users: Check the volume control. It may be a small speaker next to the clock (double-click to open), or go to Start | Settings | Control Panel | Multimedia. There you can adjust both the volume and the mixer, which is the sound quality.

7. If you still don't have sound, find the test program for your sound card. Usually, it's part of the software and in the Start menu. Run this program as a diagnostic. If the sound card is missing, reinstall the sound-card software.

Sound Unsatisfactory

Remember, this ain't no fancy stereo setup, so don't expect the same sound, Mozart. But you should be able to hear noise without pointing your ears forward.

1. If you can hear any little bit of sound, at least you know that the sound card is working. Go to Control Panel | Sound and turn up the volume. Most control panels have a separate volume for playing CDs and another one for system sounds. Adjust the correct one or your eardrum will be blasted every time you hit the wrong letter.

2. If that's not enough, check the speaker setup:

• Are speakers plugged into the computer but not into a power source? (Hello?) Is the speaker amp turned on?

• Most PCs have several jacks on the back of the computer, and a lot of people have them mixed up. Check that the speakers are plugged into Speaker Out and not Line Out or Microphone In. Line Out is meant to run sound through a stereo. Speaker Out, which is for use with PC speakers, is more amplified, and could damage your stereo. The diagram in the manual should indicate which is which, but if you have thrown out the manual and don't know jack about which jack is which, try one at a time. Make sure your ears are cleaned and that the volume is turned up high enough so that you can hear the results.

• If you have external speakers connected to a sound card, turn the volume-control knob up at least halfway and turn on the amplifier switch if there is one. Or, on most sound cards, there is a volume-control knob on the rear of the computer. Make sure that this is turned all the way up. If there is no indicator, try adjusting the knob in both directions and be prepared to stick your fingers quickly into your ears.

3. Maybe, just maybe, the program can't be turned louder. Thought of that?

Only Some Programs Produce Sound

Windows 3.X users: What kind of sound card do you have? If it is manufactured by Creative Labs or is SoundBlaster compatible, find out what type of SoundBlaster it is compatible with. Then try to set up the program to work with it. If that fails, contact the program manufacturer and ask how to set up the program with your type of sound card.

Windows 95/98 users: A sound card from an older Windows system may not work at all with Windows 95/98 or any newer system. If so, you need a new sound card. If you can't install it yourself, have someone at the computer store do it. (It should cost under $100.)

Intermittent Sound

If both the hard drive and CD-ROM are working, but sounds are fading in and out, your system is just too slow to produce the sound. Upgrade the processor or the hard drive, or get a faster CD-ROM drive (which won't help audio CDs but will help a system CD). Additional RAM may help, too. RAM can cost from $50 to $100, a new hard drive from $150 to $350, and a processor from $150 to $700.

Other Sounds Work but You Cannot Play an Audio CD

Make sure that your CD-ROM drive is working. Using the headphones you use to play a small radio, plug into the one-eighth-inch headphone jack on the CD-ROM. If you can hear sound through the headphones but not through speakers connected to your sound card, then see chapter 25, "Getting the Best Service."

Tell the repair technician that you need an internal CD audio cable. This should be a low-cost repair.

Chapter Seventeen

Laptop Techniques

One general tip about your laptop: Keep it plugged in even when it's not turned on. That will create a constant flow of power, which will prevent the battery from draining. Then, when you need your laptop, it will be charged and ready.

Can't Find Battery

Every laptop is like a small custom computer, and each is designed a little bit differently. The way the technical-design staff has fun is by playing hide the battery—each manufacturer has a sort of "secret handshake." Toshiba always puts batteries on the bottom, IBM tucks them on the bottom or under the keyboard, and Apple stows them at the front of the case, on the right- or left-hand side.

If you have some other brand, look on the bottom or on the side. The compartment is usually rectangular or oval, about the size of a pack of cigarettes, with a button to push or a latch to pull to get it open. Most of them are located near where the AC cord plugs in.

Battery Won't Charge

Remember what we said about eliminating the obvious? If the battery can't be charged, it's time for you to move on. Get a new one.

Won't Turn On

1. If you've got the machine working from wall power, first rule out the Stupid Human Tricks (see page 64) and then follow the instructions to check the fan (see pages 65–66). If your laptop continues to be unresponsive:
2. All laptops have two sources of power. One is the battery, the other is an external AC power supply (a cord with a transformer) that charges the battery. If the laptop doesn't turn on, assume that the problem may be with either of these power sources.
3. To check the AC adapter, first eject the internal battery. (See "Can't Find Battery" on page 149 if you have a problem.) If you're not sure how to eject it, refer to your manual. Then reconnect the AC power plug. If the computer doesn't start up, reset the power circuit:
   • Disconnect the external power supply and find the reset button. There's one somewhere on almost every laptop—and it's almost always hard to find. Look in the rear of the computer, on the sides, or near the power connector for a small button or a small hole large enough to stick a paper clip into.

   You'll see a small triangular symbol, or, if your karma is working, you'll actually see the words "Reset Button." (If you still can't find it, try looking in your manual or calling the manufacturer.)
   • With a paper clip, push the reset button and don't release it for at least thirty seconds.

• Now reconnect the external power supply and try again to start the computer. If it still won't start, you may have a problem with the external AC power supply. (Battery should still be disconnected.) Buy a new power adapter at a local computer store. It will cost $100 to $200, but if it doesn't help, you can return it. Or, find a rental shop that has the same power supply, and test it on a duplicate of your model. Most stores will help you with this.

4. If the computer works fine with the AC power adapter, but not with the battery, then the problem is the battery. With the advent and spread of wireless technology, new chain stores that sell only batteries have opened. Go to one if you have any trouble locating a particular battery. But before you buy a new one, pay (about $5) to test your current battery to see if it's bad.

5. If your problem is neither the power adapter nor the battery, you have a serious hardware problem with your laptop. See chapter 25, "Getting the Best Service."

Doesn't Recognize PC Card

Make sure that you haven't tried to insert your Visa card rather than your PC card. Then reinstall software.

Can't Eject PC Card

Mac users: Macs have an automatic eject. In the unlikely event that it doesn't come out automatically, and if the icon shows on the desktop, drag it to the trash as if you were ejecting a floppy.

Then, next to the socket where card pops in, there is a tiny hole. Bend a paper clip and insert it into the hole. This will trigger a spring mechanism that will pop the card out.

Windows 95/98 users: Go to your Control Panel | PC Card control panel. Select your card and hit Stop. Then try ejecting your PC card. If that doesn't work, you need professional help.

Doesn't Show Network or Get Dial Tone

Perform the procedures in "Doesn't Recognize PC Card" on page 151. If your software seems to be accessing the card, but the above problems persist, you probably need to replace the adapter that goes from the card to the jack. Contact the card manufacturer.

No Video

1. If you get a power light, but no video and no sound, reset the power circuit. (See "Won't Turn On" on page 150.)
2. If that does not work, you have a serious hardware failure most likely caused by a power problem or the motherboard. See chapter 25, "Getting the Best Service." The good news is that your hard drive is likely to be fine and all your data is safe.

Video Problems

In most cases, a laptop video problem will require professional servicing. But you might want to hook up to an external monitor in order to get your files backed up onto disks (if necessary) and keep working temporarily.

Most laptops have an external video port that allows you to connect to a regular computer monitor. You usually have to press a key sequence to redirect the video to the external monitor. See your manual for instructions.

If your screen doesn't work and an external monitor doesn't work, your problem is not a video problem. Your laptop needs servicing.

Picture Dim

Connect an external monitor as described in the preceding section. If the picture on the external monitor is clear, disconnect it. Then try adjusting the contrast and brightness settings on your laptop.

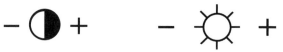

External Video Port Doesn't Work

Connect an external monitor as described in "Video Problems" on page 152. If the picture on an external monitor seems just as poor as on the laptop screen, you have a laptop-video problem that needs servicing. Laptop-screen replacements usually run about $600, but there are companies that will repair laptops for $200 to $300. If you want to find out where to go to get your laptop serviced, check our Web site, www.geeksquad.com, call us at 1-800-GEEK-SQUAD (433-5778), or see chapter 25, "Getting the Best Service."

Parts of Screen Don't Work or Are Blacked Out

See preceding section.

Blacked-Out Screen

Make sure that the computer display is set for the LCD screen and not for an external monitor. (See your manual for the instructions.)

If that's not the problem, try to connect an external monitor as described in "Video Problems" on page 152. If the picture on the external monitor is good but you get no picture at all on your laptop, you may simply have a burned-out bulb or loose wire. (The LCD screen is lit by small fluorescent bulbs.) See chapter 25, "Getting the Best Service." A loose wire would cost about $100; replacing the bulb would be $300 to $1,000. Parts may be hard to get.

Tell the repair technician that you think the problem is probably a burned-out bulb or loose wire (and pray that it's the wire).

Keyboard Not Working

A client called in a crisis. He'd spilled Coke on his laptop keyboard and was to make a presentation in twenty minutes. We saved his day. We just told him something he didn't know—that all laptops can accept an external keyboard. He borrowed one, and did the presentation. (He got the job, too, but we can't take credit for that.)

You may believe that your laptop is monogamous when it comes to keyboards, but take another look. We guarantee that you'll find an icon indicating where another keyboard could be plugged in. If you can't find it, check your manual to see where it is.

We remind everyone that in any business setting today, you're probably not more than five hundred yards from a keyboard. If you're at a hotel that brags about its customer service, getting a keyboard should be simple. If they say they don't have one, remind them that they surely do, at their very own reservations desk. This is your chance to see how far they are willing to go to please you.

To determine the cause of a laptop keyboard problem, start by plugging in an external keyboard. If you can't borrow one, go to a computer store and try one there.

- If the other keyboard works, you know that your laptop keyboard needs to be replaced. See chapter 25, "Getting the Best Service." Your cost should be about $100.
- If the external keyboard does not work, check your laptop for a virus by running your antivirus software. If no virus shows up, take your laptop for professional help and report what you've found. See chapter 25, "Getting the Best Service."

If your keyboard problem is related to a particular key, you will find the solution in chapter 11, "Calming the Keyboard."

Trackball Goes on Strike

1. If the trackball refuses to obey, first try connecting another trackball or an external mouse to the machine. If either of those works, your trackball probably just needs a cleaning. Use a tweezers or poking tool, not a cotton swab (which may leave fibers), and pay special attention to the rollers surrounding the trackball.
2. If the external mouse doesn't work and/or cleaning doesn't help, you may have a software problem. Locate the disk that came with the computer and reinstall the trackball software.
3. If you're still having problems, check your control panels. You may find a mouse control panel that tests the trackball buttons to make sure that they're working.
4. If all else fails, see chapter 25, "Getting the Best Service."

Tell the repair technician that you think the trackball assembly may need to be replaced. The cost should be around $75.

Trackpad Doesn't Work/Cursor Is Jumpy

The cause is moisture on the pad. The finger you are using to manipulate the cursor (not to be confused with the finger that occasionally *is* the curser) may be sweating. Are you nervous? Put a piece of paper between your finger and the pad.

Won't Go to Sleep

Reading it a bedtime story won't help. Try the following:
1. If you've been transferring files from laptop to desktop or network, make sure that file sharing is off.
2. Check that the Stay Awake or Don't Rest option isn't checked, under Power Book Control in Macs and Power Management in PCs.
3. Make sure that external monitor is off.
4. Try to recall if you requested folder sizes to be calculated. A PowerBook will wake up periodically to do it.

Traveling with Your Laptop

- Any time your laptop leaves the premises, you increase the chance that it may be damaged. Make sure that you are covered by a warranty.
- Back up all of the material in your laptop. (C'mon, we've told you this a million times.)
- Make sure that your insurance is in place in case the machine is stolen or lost. Your household insurance may or may not cover a laptop outside your home. If not, you may be able to purchase a rider that will do the job for a modest amount. Check with your insurance company.
- A laptop carrier should have a strap that prevents it from falling out of the case (see "Desktop vs. Laptop" on page 26). In some cases, we recommend a leash connecting the laptop to its owner.
- Airport officials will often check a laptop to make sure that it isn't just a cleverly disguised shipping container for an undesirable item such as a bomb. To speed up your trip through security, put your laptop in sleep

mode, the power-saver that shuts off everything except the brain. You can choose Sleep manually, or simply fold the cover closed without hitting the power key, which trips a sleep switch—not unlike the way your refrigerator light goes on and off. When the laptop is in this mode and you're ready to start working, you don't have to wait one or two minutes for a bootup. If a security inspection is required, you can simply flip the lid, press the space bar or mouse button, and your screen will come to life without delay. Afterward, simply close the computer. Note that a laptop with a charged battery can stay in sleep mode for several weeks.

• The information on your laptop cannot be disturbed by an X-ray machine, but while it's being checked, you may become the target of a "lap-jacking." As your laptop goes through the machine, one thief creates the diversion that holds up the line, and his accomplice makes off with your laptop as it comes out of the machine. Keep your eye on your machine at all times and stay alert for this sort of scam.

• If you're traveling to another country, consider buying a power converter for the country you're going to. You can usually get these at Radio Shack for about $100. Don't save money by buying a cheaper model—it may damage your laptop.

• A kit that provides all of the connections you need to hook up your modem to a hotel's phone system is very helpful, because some hotels make the procedure a big problem. Get the kit at Radio Shack or any other electronics retailer.

• When you check into a hotel, ask whether or not you can hook up your modem. Hooking up in some situations may damage your computer.

• When the hotel requires you to precede your call with a 9, dial 9 and then a comma (which makes a half-second pause) before dialing your number.

Nationwide Internet services can provide local numbers for you to call from wherever you are located. If you log on with AT&T or America Online, you can save yourself the hotel surcharges for long-distance calls.

Making a Presentation

At any price, you can find devices that help you produce road shows with your computer. For thousands of dollars, you can rent or buy liquid-crystal display panels (like the screen on your laptop) that go on overhead projectors and hook up to computers that project visuals and sounds. For a couple of hundred dollars you can get a scan converter that transforms signals from the laptop into TV signals and bumps sound from your computer as well. This allows you to hook your laptop to a TV of any size and make a presentation. On some newer laptops, this feature is built in. The converter itself is usually very small, and you're limited only by the size of whatever monitor you can rent or buy.

Chapter Eighteen

Application/Software Problems

When you run into a problem in this area, start by figuring out whether the cause is the computer, a specific document, or the program itself. If other programs are working properly, the computer is not the source of the problem. If a particular document is giving you a hard time, close it and open or create a new one. If you're still having trouble, your problem is with the application/software itself. A part of the program has become corrupt, something that happens from time to time in political systems and computer programs.

The solution is to reinstall the program from the original disks. The reinstallation will overwrite what's already there, but if that doesn't do the trick, delete (uninstall) the program and *then* reinstall it.

If the problem persists, contact the software manufacturer by phone or Web site. The telephone number for the tech support should be in the manual that came with your software or on the company's Web site. If you don't know the Web address, entering www.companyname.com may get you there. Tell the tech support person what steps you've tried and you'll probably be able to get help. If not, try an outside source of help (such as the Geek Squad at www.geeksquad.com or 1-800-GEEK-SQUAD [433-5778]).

Can't Install Software or Upgrade

Run out of space?

1. You may not have enough room on your hard drive to install new software. Ten percent (or more) of the total room on your hard drive should always be unused. Here's how to check how much hard-drive space you've used and how much is available:

Mac users: Select Hard Drive | Get Info.

Windows 95/98 users: Select My Computer | Drive | Properties. You will see a pie chart with the information that you need.

2. It's also possible you don't have enough RAM for the particular program you want. Look in the manual for the specification requirements, and then check to see what's on your computer:

Mac users: Select Apple | Control Panel | Memory.

Windows 95/98 users: Select My Computer | Control Panel | System | Performance.

3. The software may not be compatible with your computer. This is probably the case if the computer locks up or crashes during installation. Check with the software manufacturer.

When buying software:
- If you don't see a technical-support number on the software package, reconsider whether this is something you really want to buy. Good software companies support what they produce. If the company isn't there to help make the installation easy, how good can the product be?
- Just because you see the words "Compatible with Windows" or "Compatible with Macintosh" on the box doesn't mean it's so. Check with the dealer.
- Some obvious, but oft-ignored advice: Read the manual if you're having installation problems. If the product doesn't come with a manual, return it.

Software Locks Up/Freezes

1. Is the problem with one particular document? Are you having a problem, for example, opening up or printing a single Microsoft Word document? Try creating another document. If the new one isn't a problem, though the original continues to be, see chapter 19, "Document/File Dilemmas."
2. Does the application lock up in more than one document? Then see "Uninstalling/Reinstalling Application Software" on page 162. Use the original disks and follow the instructions.

Can't Print from Application

Once you select Print, does the screen look similar to the way it looks when you print in other applications? Does it report printing activity the way it does when you print in other applications? If not, the program may need its own printer configuration. Check the manual for the program to see the instructions regarding the printer.

Mac: Bomb Appears When You Pick a Different Font

The font has been corrupted. (This is the risk you take when you allow the Ding-bats to hang around with the Palatinos without some kind of supervision.) Reinstall font from original disk.

Mac: Application Frequently "Unexpectedly Quits"

Increase the memory allocation: Click on the application (such as Microsoft Word), then on the Get Info option under the File menu. Increase the memory size in the Minimum box to what it says in the Suggested box. If the problem persists, reinstall the software.

Uninstalling/Reinstalling Application Software

Many times, if you're having problems with an application, we just recommend a simple reinstallation of the application software.

Always remove the current version of the software, if possible, before you reinstall it, as follows:

Mac users: Simply drag the program and all its associated files into the trash. Then install just as you did the first time.

Windows 3.X users: In the same area that you find the icon for the program, you may also find the Uninstall program. If no Uninstall option is available, just reinstall the application without removing the prior version. This should fix the problem.

Windows 95/98 users: Go to Start | Settings | Control Panel | Remove Programs. Click on the program and click Remove. Reinstall the software.

If reinstallation doesn't help, see chapter 25, "Getting the Best Service."

Tell the repair technician what you've done and say that you think your problem is caused by an operating system error or some remnants of the application that are lingering in the system.

Identifying Software Version

Mac users: Open the program. Click on the Apple icon in the upper-left-hand corner of the screen. Click on About [name of program] and you'll see a screen that IDs the version that you're using.

Windows users: Go to the Help screen and look up the version number. Or check for the version number on the startup screen when you open the application.

Chapter Nineteen

Document/File Dilemmas

Is the problem you're having with the program or with a particular document? (Just so you don't get confused, whether we're talking about a document or a file, we're talking about the same thing: a piece of work that you've created in a particular program.) If you can open or create another document within the program, then you know the program itself is okay. Next try putting the document on a floppy and inserting it into another computer. If it's still not readable, you know problem is with the document itself.

Try to "import" it into a similar program. For example, if you have a damaged WordPerfect document, try opening it within the latest version of Microsoft Word. Most newer versions of word processing and spreadsheet software can import many different document formats. In some cases, a damaged document that won't open in Microsoft Word will open in in Excel. Excel is designed to import text into a spreadsheet, so it may not be so fussy about whether the document is perfect. It may overlook the damaged areas that cause your program to crash whenever you try to access the document.

Problems Transferring Files

See chapter 24, "Computer-to-Computer Communication."

Problems Converting Files

See chapter 24, "Computer-to-Computer Communication."

Problems Finding a File

When creating letters and spreadsheets, you save the file and may print it out, but you may not be giving a lot of thought to where that file is held in the computer. Weeks or months later, you may have trouble finding it. Fortunately, most computers have a feature that will help you search. Though the following explains how to search for a particular word, the Find option may also allow you to search by other cues, such as a date.

> **Mac users:** Find File is under the File menu. Also, typing the key command Apple+F will bring up a window for you to type in the word that you're searching for.

> **Windows 3.X users:** Choose Main | File Manager | File | Search. Type in the word that you're trying to locate.

> **Windows 95/98 users:** Under the Start menu, you'll see an option called Find. Choose Files or Folders. Type in the word that you're searching for.

When using this feature, people commonly make the mistake of typing in the entire name of the file—or what they believe to be the entire name. Many times, if you have made a typo or a spelling error, then you're searching for the wrong name. Our friend, for instance, searched in vain for "Income Tax," only to discover, when it occurred to him to search for "Income" alone, that he had created a file named "Income Sex." (Where

could his mind have been?) Try searching for a portion of a name, just in case you've mistyped or misspelled what you're looking for.

If you still can't find the file, a disk-utility program like Norton Utilities includes a Find File feature that's easy to use and has extra features to aid a search. If you don't remember the exact file name, it will allow you to search by creation date, modification date, and other methods.

File Deleted in Error

You've just clicked OK and agreed to delete a file that you had absolutely no intention of deleting. (Can you tell us today's date? What city you're in? The name of the current president?) If you act quickly, you have a very good chance of getting that file back.

Do not open any other programs or create any new files—the more you use your computer after you've deleted a file, the more you reduce your likelihood of rescuing the lost file. If you have already installed a disk-utility program (such as Norton Utilities), look for a feature called Unerase. This software actually stores files that you've recently deleted. The sooner you run it after deleting a file, the better your chances of recovering it.

CAUTION: If you do not have a utilities program and decide to get one now, do not install the software on your computer at this point. That may overwrite the still-existing deleted file, dooming your chance of recovery. Instead, install the utilities program on a second computer (or find a computer in which it's been installed) and copy the Unerase portion onto a floppy disk. Then run Unerase from the floppy disk. It will check your hard drive for the missing file.

File Cannot Be Opened

The file is in there, but the little men inside the computer are holding it hostage. You get a message that the document is corrupt or that you can't open it. Or the computer simply locks up.

1. If you can see the file, try to make a copy of it. Under the File menu, choose Copy or Duplicate and give the copied file a different name. Then try to open the copy.
2. If that doesn't work, use Microsoft Word to peer into the file. If you don't have Word, take the disk with the problematic file to a business center such as Kinko's, where they have Microsoft Word. Open that application. Get into Microsoft Word | File | Open. Before you select a document, go to the box labeled List Files of Type and click on All Files, Text Only, or ASCII Text. Then select the file. Even if the file is a spreadsheet or a database file, Microsoft Word will let you see if your data is inside the file. It may appear jumbled, but it will be in there. The garbage that you're seeing is hidden file information—a type of header—that your program used to identify and format the type of file.
3. Scan through the document, leaving pertinent information and deleting any foreign characters. Though time consuming, this is the quickest way to reconstruct a corrupted file. Once you've pieced it together as best you can, choose Save As. Then, under Save File as Type, select the format you want. Now you should be able to open the file from your program. For problems with specific file types, like database or spreadsheet files, see chapter 20, "Recovering Data."

Mac: Application Is Missing

The computer tells you that the application that created a document is missing or cannot be found.

1. If you know that the application is there, the problem is that the invisible Desktop (the database that manages everything, the power behind the throne) has been damaged. Rebuild the Desktop by pressing Command+Option as you restart your Mac. Click OK when the prompt asks if you want to rebuild the Desktop. The thermometer window will appear, then soon disappear, and you should be able to continue with no problem.
2. If that doesn't work, click on the SimpleText program. (It comes with the Apple operating system.) Then try to open the document within that program.

Mac: Processing Is Slow

If copying files or opening big folders takes a long time, rebuild the Desktop: Restart the machine, holding down Command+Option. Follow the prompts. This gets rid of files that you've already deleted but that the Desktop keeps around for a while.

Mac: Calls for Ejected Disk

The disk is gone. But the machine keeps asking for it anyway. It's a little poignant, but still . . . Keep pressing Command+. [period] until the command stops appearing.

Lost Password on a File

See "Password Forgotten" on page 196.

Chapter Twenty

Recovering Data

Limiting Damage in an Emergency

When the machine freezes, you may be able to save all or part of the data in the document you're working on by shutting down the computer properly. Follow these steps:

1. Wait a minute or two to make certain that the machine is frozen, not just moving slowly. Then, in order, check the following:
2. A keyboard or mouse cable may have become loose. Make sure that the cable is plugged in all the way.
3. Check for other observable clues. If you hear anything, you know that the hard drive is accessing files, which may be causing a delay. A blinking light may indicate that the computer is engaged in some other, delaying activity. Maybe it's just taking a little break. Wait another five to seven minutes before proceeding.

4. Shut down all external devices, such as external modems, scanners, and printers. Wait ten seconds, then power them back on. That may reset one of these devices, which in turn will reset the computer. If not, continue . . .

5. Manually eject any floppy and/or CD-ROM disks that are in place.

Mac users: There is a small hole below the slot where you insert the disk. Insert the end of a paper clip about two inches straight into the hole. If you push in hard enough, you will activate a spring mechanism and the floppy will be ejected. See your computer manual if this isn't clear.

Windows users: PCs are equipped with a manual eject button.

6. Try a "warm reboot." This means restarting without shutting the computer down manually, by using the computer's Restart command on the computer. You may lose data, but you will at least be able to restart the computer.

Mac users: Try the "Vulcan Nerve Pinch": Simultaneously hit the keys Apple+Option+Escape. When the dialogue box asks if you want to "force quit," choose Yes. If the freeze is in the application, and the machine begins to operate normally, try to save your files quickly. If the freeze is not in the application, you probably won't be able to do anything. In either case, continue to step 7.

RIGHT FOOT, "COMMAND"
LEFT HAND, "OPTION"
LEFT FOOT, "ESC"

Windows users: Simultaneously hit Control+Alt+Delete. If you're lucky, this will reboot the computer. If not, continue to step 7.

7. Shut the computer off.
8. Wait ten seconds, then turn the computer back on. Running a disk-utility program (see "Checkups," page 59) before running any other programs may recover any lost data before you proceed with normal use. If you don't already have one, go out and get one. People often buy disk-utility programs after a freeze, so they're made to help out in this kind of situation.

THE FIRST TIME

I can still
feel it
in my stomach,
the coldness of my skin . . .
the day—
no; it was night—
when I
pressed
the keyboard key,
the one they keep
far to the right
so no one
will confuse it with Page Up and Number Lock
and Clear.
I pressed that key,
the one that had
for so, so many days
brought
me in touch
with
life and
like

and
being, too—
and
pressed
and pressed
and it
brought
nothing
but
the
empty sound of
plastic
tapping
plastic.
Click,
it said.
Click,
it said.
Click and *click* and *click.*
The tears were streaming down my face.
My monitor was black.
My passage to the world was closed.
I was once again
alone.
Click and *click* and *click* and *click*
click and *click* and *click* . . .
Sometimes when I am tired
and things are going bad
the nightmare
comes back
and haunts me
but nothing's like the first
time
that my computer
crashed.

      —Martha Rose Reeves

Reports "Document Cannot Be Read"

If you have saved the file to a floppy, copy it to the hard drive and then try to read it.

If your file is already on the hard drive, run a disk-repair utility such as Scan-Disk or Disk First Aid and see if that can recover the file.

Whenever you have a problem with a floppy disk (or any file on that disk), never trust it again. No second chances. Move any and all files from that floppy onto another floppy or, preferably, onto a hard drive. Once you have recovered your data, get rid of it as soon as possible. This is a good time to remind you never to work directly from a floppy. Copy your files onto the hard drive before you work on them.

Getting to Data After a Crash

Your system automatically saves data while it's working on it. After a crash, files called temp files appear. These documents, with "temp" or "TMP" in the name, are backups of the data that you were working on at the time of the crash. You don't see them normally, because when you leave a program, the computer deletes all those files. But if you don't leave normally, it can't delete them because it didn't close normally.

Mac users with Systems 7.5 and later: After a crash, when you restart, in the trash, you will find a folder called "Rescued items from [name of hard drive]." Those are the temp files, and they stay there until you delete them. Try to find these immediately, transfer them out of the trash, and rename them or copy them into another document.

Windows 95/98 users: Temp files are under C:\windows\temp.

Your data will definitely be lost only if the floppy disk you were working on is badly damaged or part of the information on the hard drive has become "corrupted"—destroyed or damaged—because of something physically wrong with the drive or because of a virus infection. Generally, your chances of getting back all your data are fifty-fifty.

If You Had No Backup

In a data-recovery crisis, when you can't recover the files from the hard drive or a floppy disk and have no backup, you still have some cause for hope.

Disk Editors

A disk-editor program like Disk Edit, which is included with Norton Utilities, may be of some use in recovering your data. Such programs work sort of like a magnifying glass, allowing you to see parts of the disk, and may permit you to recover some of the data in chunks. It's a crude process, but it may help. However, if used incorrectly, disk editors can damage other data that hasn't been affected by your crash, so if you are not comfortable with using an editor, have a professional help you.

Using a Printout

If you have a printout of the lost material in a clear, typed format, a scanner could save the day. New scanning software includes optical character recognition (OCR) that can turn text into an electronic format—that is, a computer file—even if there are some markings on it. (See "Scanning for Beginners" on page 119.) With this technique, we have helped a client whose computer crashed while she was working on a Ph.D. dissertation. If you don't own a scanner, bring the printout to a business center, such as Kinko's. Or fax it over. Their personnel may be able to convert the material to a disk by the time you arrive at the store.

If you don't have a scanner, a fax machine might be the solution. See "Scanning Without a Scanner" on page 120.

Note that scanned material is only about 95 percent accurate, and accuracy

depends heavily on the quality of the original images. To make it perfect again, you will probably have to correct the formatting (things like underlining and bold, for instance) and use Spell Check in your new file. So get ready to proofread.

Retyping

If you have a lengthy hard copy, consider hiring a temp service to reenter the data. While this may seem expensive and a little old-fashioned, once you have lost a certain volume of data, it may be the most cost-effective solution. Also, this process is *guaranteed* to work, whereas data-recovery techniques take time and results aren't 100 percent certain.

Getting Professional Help

Before you go to a data-recovery expert, ask for help from a local computer-service shop. They can often handle a recovery job, and frequently do it at lower cost than a firm that specializes in this work. Such a company may bill from $250 to several thousands of dollars, depending on the nature and size of the problem (and the nature and size of the gonads of the person setting the fee)—but there are times when a person needs data recovered at any cost.

Of the professional firms specializing in using complex voodoo to solve very difficult data-recovery situations, two of the best on the planet are DriveSavers and Ontrack. They're expensive, but they can often work miracles. (See Appendix D, "Resources.")

Chapter Twenty-one

Using the Internet

Choosing a Provider

Many people are confused by the difference between an Internet service provider (ISP) and services such as AOL. Here's the skinny: They're the same thing. Any company that lets you establish an e-mail account or get into the World Wide Web (WWW) is an Internet service provider. AOL is an ISP. So is AT&T.

There are two parts to Internet access. The first is a piece of software that dials the modem into the ISP. This software is usually provided by AOL, Netscape, or whoever your ISP might be. In newer computers, it is built into your operating system.

The second part of the process is the application that you use to go from site to site on the Internet. It's called a browser. Netscape and Internet Explorer are the most popular. Any ISP will work with any browser, but if you started with Netscape and then downloaded Explorer, don't keep both on your machine. (See "Uninstalling/Reinstalling Application Software" on page 162 for information on how to remove software.) Pick one and stay with it. Otherwise, you might mess up your e-mail and generate other conflicts.

Even people who are already on the Internet may find these tips helpful:

• Stick with a well-known brand name when you're selecting an Internet provider. These companies tend to offer better service and better technical support, and you're less likely to get a busy signal from them.
• Choose a flat-rate service, which will allow you to dial in and stay connected for an unlimited amount of time for both e-mail and World Wide Web access. You should pay no more than $25 per month.
• Any software you need should be provided free of charge.
• Look for a customer-support line open 24/7. It's rare, but one place that does provide such a service is AT&T WorldNet. (If you call 1-800-World-Net at any time of the day, they'll walk you through your problem. At this writing, there doesn't seem to be too long a wait.)

Trouble Connecting

1. Check the phone line to make sure that your phone or an extension isn't off the hook.
2. If the provider won't take your password, check that you're typing the user name or password in the exact upper- and lowercase letters that appear on your account information sheet, because these things are case-sensitive. If you don't know what yours should be, call and have the customer-service person recite the letters in upper- and lowercase to verify the spelling.
3. If correct retyping doesn't solve the problem, call the provider to make sure your account is still active.

4. When installing your software, make sure that you get the message saying, "The installation was completed successfully."

5. Make sure that you're using an up-to-date version of the software. An outdated version could be so obsolete that it's unusable.

6. When the main line is constantly busy, most providers start using alternate numbers. They don't volunteer these numbers, but will provide them if you call.

7. A line that is constantly busy is an indication that your provider is on overload. Consider switching to another company.

8. If you're having trouble dialing out of a hotel, see "Traveling with Your Laptop" on page 156.

Images Slow to Appear

When this happens, it means, basically, that you need to do some housekeeping by clearing your cache—cleaning out files that are slowing the machine down. Cache files are created so that if you return to a site, it will reload more quickly. But often the site has changed since you were there last, so you'll probably have to reload anyway.

Mac users: For both Netscape and Internet Explorer, select Preferences | Clear Cache.

Windows users: If using Netscape, click Preferences | Clear Cache. If using Microsoft Internet Explorer, click Control Panel | Internet | Clear Cache.

Sending and Receiving E-Mail on the Road

With the right setup, you can access e-mail, just like voice mail, from anywhere at anytime. Here are two easy ways:

• America Online is so universal that once you set up an account, you should have no problem finding a computer loaded with AOL software that will allow you access to your own e-mail. Just replace the existing account name with yours and dial away. To keep your e-mail private, don't save your password on the borrowed machine.

• An increasingly popular way to access e-mail is to use a free e-mail service via the World Wide Web directly. Yahoo offers the best of them. Go to www.yahoo.com and click on the Free E-Mail button. This allows you to access e-mail from anywhere, anytime, using any computer that can access and view a Web page. Once you enter your e-mail address and password at Yahoo's mail site, you'll be able to read the e-mail sent to you at that address, compose new e-mail, and even save your e-mail in special folders. (The password keeps other people from peeking into your mailbox.) This is extremely convenient and should be checked out by anyone who travels. When you come home and check your mail, it will all be there.

Sending and Receiving E-Mail Without Internet Access

Call Juno (1-800-564-JUNO). They'll send you a disk (containing software) that you install to get free e-mail. (You will need a modem, too.) Shipping charges will be about $10. Or, visit our site on the Web at www.geeksquad.com and download our software for free.

Sending Files

If you have an Internet provider, you can use the Internet to send spreadsheets, letter documents, or graphics—or all three—to anyone with an e-mail address. However, if the file is bigger than five megabytes, the process will be time consuming. You might be better off sending the disk by mail.

There are two ways to incorporate another file into your e-mail document:

• After you open your e-mail and compose a message, select a command under the File menu called Attach File. Follow the computer prompts

to find the file on your hard drive and attach it to your e-mail.

• Go to your word-processing program and copy the text, then paste it directly into the e-mail. When you do it this way, your e-mail document won't keep the formatting—so bold type, underlining, and so on won't show up. However, while the newest versions of word-processing programs can read documents made by other word-processing programs, older versions may not have this capacity. If the person you're communicating with can't open your attachment, copying and pasting may be your only option.

If you have trouble opening an attachment that has been sent to you, don't try to open it from your browser. Contact the person who has sent you the e-mail or revisit the site from which you downloaded it to find out what program created the attachment. You'll have to use that program, or a program that will convert that file to a compatible format, to open it.

Not all e-mail systems allow you to attach files. If you are planning to use this method while traveling, it's best to ask in advance if the Internet provider you will be using has a system that supports file attachments.

Credit-Card Protection

Any time you're going to buy anything on the Web, deal only with sites that are secure—sites that use data encryption. A credit-card number sent to such a site cannot be intercepted and used by an unauthorized person. A key or padlock icon in the lower-left-hand corner of the browser window indicates that the site uses encryption. If the key is broken or the padlock is open, the site is not secure. A prompt may warn you about this.

Once you enter your information on a Web site, it should then generate a confirmation screen. Sometimes a confirmation will be e-mailed to you. Print this out and keep it for your records.

Never submit your credit-card number via e-mail. This is not secure and no company should ever ask you to use this method of payment.

Surfing the Net

Search engines are the key to finding anything on the Internet. Some, such as Yahoo, have humans doing the categorizing, whereas others, like HotBot and Dogpile, gather information mechanically. So, if you ask Yahoo about "Heat," you could look under sports and get all sorts of information about the Miami basketball team. If you ask Dogpile, you would get information about the weather as well as about the team. Because Dogpile and HotBot are search engines that search other search engines, they can give you a tremendous number of responses, but if your search inquiry is broad, the amount may be bewildering.

Some of the most popular search engines are:

Getting on the Web

AltaVista (www.altavista.digital.com)
Excite (www.excite.com)
HotBot (www.hotbot.com)
Lycos (www.lycos.com)
Yahoo! (www.yahoo.com)

While each engine will instruct you on its own specifics, basically you just type in a word or phrase and the engine tries to find references at sites around the Web. Test the various search engines to see where you're most comfortable, and remember, when you can't find something on one, do not hesitate to look via another. To help you get the information you want, the key is not what you say, but how you say it—sometimes just altering a few words will get you different results. AltaVista, for example, asks you to put your inquiry in the form of a question. "What is the Stanley Cup?" may get a slightly different group of documents than "How big is the Stanley Cup?"

How you link words is also very important when using search engines. Following are some tips on how this works, but click on the Help button in whatever search engine you're using and you'll get more suggestions.

- "and": Type in *apple and pie,* and the engine will look for all sites containing both words. A plus sign will have the same effect *(apple + pie).*
- "or": Type in *apple or pie,* and the engine will look for all sites containing either topic.
- "near": Type in *apple near pie,* and the engine will find the sites where those words are near one another. (Each engine defines "near" in a slightly different though specific way. One search engine defines "near" as any usage when there are no more than one hundred words separating the two words you are looking for.)
- "not": Type in *apple and pie not cinnamon,* and the engine will look for all sites related to the first two but exclude the third. A minus sign will have the same effect *(apple and pie - cinnamon).*
- Quote marks (" "): Type in *cinnamon and apple and pie,* and you might get millions of responses. But if you put quote marks around them as a single phrase—"cinnamon apple pie"—you'll get sites with that specific phrase only.
- Asterisk (*): Insert an asterisk, or "wild card," in the middle of a word or after it and you'll get searches for plurals, suffixes, and alternate spellings.

For more details, go to users.ids.net/~davehab/. You will find great advice there in *How to Search the World Wide Web: A Tutorial for Beginners and Non-Experts,* by David P. Habib and Robert L. Baillot.

Downloading

Use this technique to copy images and text from the Web to your hard drive so that you can look at them when you're not on-line:

Mac users: Drag the image from your Web browser to the desktop. If you aren't able to do this, click once on the image and go up to the File menu, choose Save As, and save it to your hard drive. Or, try copying and pasting it as you would in conventional word processing.

Windows 95/98 users: Highlight text by holding down the left button until you select what you want. Then, right click, and you can either copy or print. If you choose to copy, just open a word-processing application and hit Paste (in the Edit menu) to get the text pasted where you want it. You can also save a picture: the Save dialogue box will appear, so you can choose where to keep it.

Windows 95/98 users: Any image on the Web can be your background wallpaper. Right click on the image and a box will pop up saying, "Set as Wallpaper." This will tile the image into the background, where it remains until you change it. (We have Frank Sinatra on ours.)

The latest version of Microsoft Word will allow you to incorporate Web pages into normal word-processing documents. If you don't have it, you may have to edit the text, which may appear with strange line breaks and other quirks.

Preventing Unwanted E-Mail

Some e-mail programs have "filtering" that prevents unwanted e-mail. Check your manual, or the Help file, to see if you've got this option and, if so, how to get it running.

Controlling What the Kids Can See

It's 10:00 P.M. Do you know where your kids have been? If they've been traveling in cyberspace, there's a good chance that they've left footprints. When

one of our Special Agents did a tune-up for a customer that included clearing out a history of the Web sites that had been visited, the customer discovered that his son had been to places he shouldn't have been.

Your browser may allow you to exercise some control over the content that comes into your house and filter out what is derogatory, racist, or otherwise objectionable. Check your Options settings, or call for tech support if you can't figure out how to do it. Your service provider may also have some way of controlling the content directly.

There are also programs that you can download, like Cyberpatrol and Netnanny, that may help suppress objectionable material and track whether anyone in your house has tried to find it. The programs have to be updated periodically, though, and are not 100 percent guaranteed to keep your kids from content that you might not approve of. You've seen how clever they can be in figuring out how to avoid chores and explain bad schoolwork. You haven't seen anything yet . . .

Crashes/Lockups/Freezes While You Are on the Internet

Web browsers and sites tend to be buggier than normal programs for several reasons. One, the technology is complex. Two, the material is redone frequently. And three, hundreds of thousands of people are creating new sites. Not everyone is neat and clean about Web design.

Mac users: If your computer is crashing while on the Internet:
1. Make sure that you are using the latest version of the operating system.
2. Make sure that you have enough RAM for your Internet browser software. Try Get Info on your application and check the amount of RAM it needs. Adjust if necessary.

Browser Error Messages

Error messages say things like "DNS entry not found" or "System is not responding" or "Error type 404." They tell you that you may have incorrectly typed the name of the site, the site might be out of service at the moment, or the site may have moved. If you didn't mistype it, keep trying at various intervals, as Web sites are often down for maintenance.

"Transfer Is Interrupted"

Call waiting may create this problem. Temporarily disabling call waiting before going on-line may be an option on your system. See "Disabling Call Waiting" on page 139.

Chapter Twenty-two

When the Computer Seems to Have a Mind of Its Own

Any Odd Behavior

When the computer is acting weird in any way, sometimes it just needs your help to clear its head. Try a warm reboot, the computer equivalent of a time-out, by pushing the Restart button. This saves wear and tear on the power switch.

If the computer is frozen, you have to do a cold reboot—a fancy term for manually flipping the off switch and letting the machine cool down for half a minute or so before you flip the switch back to on. Either way, you clear the memory, which may solve the problem.

Periodic Freezes/Lockups

You call them freezes. We call them lockups. Po*ta*to, po*tah*to; they're the same thing. First, figure out what kind of lockup problem you're having by determining at which point it occurs.

System lockups occur intermittently and in no particular pattern. You may see the startup screen but you can't run any programs; at other times, the computer is sitting idle or you're using a word-processing program. If you have this problem, move down to *application lockups,* below.

Device lockups always occur when you are using a specific device, such as the printer or a scanner. To test whether it's a hardware problem, restart the computer without that device connected. If the computer works, then you've probably got an extension or driver conflict. See "Resolving Driver/Extension Conflicts–Reinstalling Drivers/Extensions" on page 213, which discusses reinstalling the driver. If that doesn't help, see chapter 25, "Getting the Best Service."

Screen freezes

Application lockups occur only when using a particular program. Otherwise, the computer works fine. See "Uninstalling/Reinstalling Application Software" on page 162.

Document lockups occur only when you are editing or modifying a particular file. In other words, Word, Excel, or any other application works fine except when you try to open or work with a particular spreadsheet or file.

1. If you can open your file at all, copy it, then open a new document and paste the contents of the misbehaving file into it.

2. If you can see your data but have a problem printing it, get access to another application, if possible, and try printing it from there. (If you're using a spreadsheet, try opening it in another spreadsheet program; try opening a word-processing document in another word-processing program.)

3. If you can't open the document at all, copy it to a floppy and try to open it on another computer.

4. Excel only: An element encoded in the program may be creating the problem. If you open your document in another program, it probably won't crash.

Computer Is Slow

We frequently got these complaints right about four-thirty, five in the afternoon, and we finally caught on. The callers aren't sweating over a word-processing or spreadsheet problem—they're kicking back to play games at the end of the day and finding that the office machines just aren't playing fast enough. Solution: Upgrade the video card. Think the boss will spring for it?

Routine Operation Gets Strange Results

1. Check for heat. If the computer case seems hot to touch or air vents emit unusual amount of heat, check to see if air is coming out of vents and that power fan (at back of computer, near power cord) is turning. If not, see chapter 25, "Getting the Best Service." Tell the repair technician that you think you have a fan problem.

2. Check for interference from other electronic devices. (See "Obey the Twelve Commandments" on page 44, specifically number 6.)

3. After ruling out possibilities 1 and 2:

   Mac users: Install and run diagnostic software, such as Norton Utilities.

   Windows users: Choose Surface Scan from your built-in ScanDisk. While it's running, listen for abnormal sounds. If any sectors of your drive are bad (which ScanDisk will tell you), you will have to replace the hard drive. See chapter 25, "Getting the Best Service."

Program Opens Other Than the One You Tried to Open

Mac users: Turn off the computer, and when you restart, rebuild the Desktop: Hold down the Apple+Option keys during startup and keep them pressed down until the prompt asks if you're sure you want to rebuild the Desktop. Click onto the box that says OK. You'll see a thermometer window, which will disappear when the job is done.

Windows users: Go to the Microsoft Web site and download RegClean. Run that program. It cleans and reorganizes the registry where all information about files and programs is kept.

Mac: Icons Look Strange

Turn off the computer, and when you restart, rebuild the Desktop: Hold down the Apple+Option keys during startup and keep them pressed down until the prompt asks if you're sure you want to rebuild the Desktop. Click onto the box that says OK. You'll see a thermometer window, which will disappear when the job is done.

CAUTION: If you're using an operating system earlier than 7.5.5, rebuilding the Desktop will erase any comments in your files' Get Info boxes, unless you rebuild the Desktop with a disk-utility program rather than with the two-key method.

Random Characters Appear

This could be a video or hard-drive issue. See chapter 25, "Getting the Best Service."

WHEN THE
COMPUTER
SEEMS TO
HAVE A MIND
OF ITS OWN
193

"Blue Screen of Death"

Windows 95/98 users: If there is a crash, Windows has a built-in feature that causes the appearance of a blue screen with a message in white at the bottom, where the computer tells you what the problem is. Even though you don't understand it (because it is written in Vulcan), record exactly what you see on the screen, letter for letter. If you call tech support, having this number may speed up the troubleshooting process. The technician may tell you to simply shut down and then restart the machine.

Mac: Trash Won't Empty

You've seen the movie: Mickey Mouse is the sorcerer's apprentice trying to empty out the basement. Similarly, your trash can stays swollen.

1. Restart the machine.
2. Or reboot from an emergency startup disk.
3. Or try a Disk First Aid.
4. Or try a Norton Utility (which will repair the folder so that it can be recognized by Trash).

Chapter Twenty-three

Security Issues

Forgotten password

Many people believe that a home computer is vulnerable to hackers on the Internet. If it's off-line, or off, no one can log into your home computer via the Internet, but there are other security matters that should concern you.

Password Forgotten

Many programs will allow you to protect your documents with a password, which is meant to deter others from accessing your information. Of course, if you forget your own password, you can't get in there, either. Check our Web site (www.geeksquad.com) to get some software that will help you find the password you have lost.

Look in the free software area, and identify the software program you're using (Microsoft Word, Microsoft Excel, FileMaker Pro). When you download the software, you will be given the number of the company that wrote it. You call them, give them your credit card over the phone (your cost will run anywhere from $50 to $200), and they'll give you the code word that is needed to run their password-cracking software. (They'll verify that you're you because you are giving them a credit-card number.)

Once you're in the software, you select the file you need and you're given your missing password.

Creating Crack-Proof Passwords

Most password-cracking programs can only crack passwords of less than fifteen characters. The longer the password, the harder it is to crack. If you want a very secure password, use the maximum number of characters a program allows. But since such a password is virtually invulnerable to cracking, be sure you know how to find it should you lose it.

Preventing Theft

- Most computers include a special port on the back for installing a security device (manufactured by a company such as Kensington) that acts like a bike lock and prevents anyone from walking off with your machine.

• Using passwords to control your operating system makes it difficult for anyone who steals your computer to get information. Both Mac and Windows have a Passwords control panel that allows you to chose a password that must be entered before the computer will start.

• You can buy commercial software that will lock and encrypt the data on your hard drive.

Removing Information from Your Computer Before You Sell It

Mac users: Erase the hard drive by initializing it with Disk First Aid. Your system is secure.

Windows 3.X users: When you're at the DOS prompt, type Format /U. That will clear the contents of your hard drive completely. Whoever purchases your computer from you cannot reformat the drive. Reinstall the operating system. (See "Total/Clean Reinstallation" on page 212.) Your system is secure.

Windows 95/98 users: Go to Start | Shut Down. Restart in MS-DOS, then click OK. Type Format /U. That will clear the contents of your hard drive completely, and whoever purchases your computer from you cannot reformat the drive. Reinstall the operating system. (See "Total/Clean Reinstallation" on page 212.) Your system is secure.

Chapter Twenty-four

Computer-to-Computer Communication

Exchanging Word-Processing Documents

Exchanging word-processing documents is a two-step process. First, the software must be made compatible (so that, for example, WordPerfect can speak to Microsoft Word), and then the operating systems must be made compatible (if you're trying to get Mac to talk to Windows).

Making the Software Compatible

If you have to trade disks with someone and you don't know what word processing they're using, your best bet is to save the document as RTF (Rich-Text Format). In this form, a document can be opened and saved to just about any word-processing application. What's more, it retains a lot of the formatting (such as bold, italic, and some indents) that are lost in many other translations.

Generally, the best software to convert word-processing documents is Microsoft Word. If you don't have the latest version, Kinko's probably does. Word's Save As menu allows you to choose many different formats, including RTF.

If you have a document from another machine that you want to open, don't just double-click on the icon—open it within the application. In other words, first click on the application (such as Microsoft Word), and then select File Open and proceed to open your document that way.

Making the Systems Compatible

• **From Mac to PC:** To make a Mac disk that can be read by a PC computer, you need a PC-formatted floppy. Copy the file onto such a disk, insert it into the PC, and open up the file within the program you're using (for example, click on Microsoft Word if it's a Microsoft Word document and open up the document through Word). If the disk is going back to a Mac user, save the text in a compatible format (Word, if it will be read by Word) or in RTF (see "Making the Software Compatible" on page 199). The Mac user will be able to insert your PC-formatted disk and read it.

• **From PC to Mac:** If you have an older Mac, you may have to go to a business center such as Kinko's, but if you have a Mac made after 1994, it can read from or write to IBM-compatible disks—floppy disks, CD-ROMs, Zip disks, and such. (But it can only copy and view individual files, not run Windows programs from a disk.) When you insert a PC-formatted disk into a Mac, there may be a brief wait before the icon shows up on your screen. When it does, open your word-processing program and click File Open. If there's a problem, you may have to identify the File Type (the program in which the document was saved), such as Excel, Lotus, or Word.

Always remember that you first have to make the software compatible, then the systems.

Exchanging Quicken Files

Quicken makes Mac to PC conversion very easy. It has an Export command in its File menu that will walk you through the process of saving your data (check history, deposit information, and so on) on a disk that another machine can read. This is a useful feature if you want to give your accountant your financial information on disks. If any changes are made, they will be retained when the disk is imported back into your machine.

Exchanging a Database

Transporting a database file, such as a mailing list, from one machine to another is a common need, and the most usual problem is figuring out what program was used to create the original file. There are two ways to do it:

- Use FileMaker Pro (available in either Windows or Mac formats), which makes it easy to import, open, and examine a database file created in just about any format.
- Contact a local mailing-list house. These firms specialize in opening oddball formats. For a couple of hundred dollars (and within minutes), it's likely that one of their experts can convert the file into a format that you can use. If you're a very effective social engineer, you may even persuade someone to do it for no cost.

Exchanging Spreadsheets

Microsoft Excel will open almost any spreadsheet known to mankind. If you don't have the latest version, bring a disk with your mystery file to a machine that does (you can probably find one at Kinko's or another business center). Open the file in Microsoft Excel using the Import command under the File menu. Scroll down the Save As menu to save your file in the version you want.

Sending/Receiving a Computer File Using a Fax

If you're communicating with someone who doesn't have access to the Internet, the next best thing is to fax your material back and forth via your computer modem. Although every new modem comes with fax software, many people don't take advantage of it. Each computer is different, so we can't give all the instructions for the setup here, but you will find it in your manual. The faxed material, which is received as a graphic, can either be printed out or translated by the software into text that you can incorporate into your document file.

Faxing can be a very useful tool for creating a paperless office because received faxes are automatically saved as files on your hard drive.

Mac users: We recommend Global Village modems. They come with the best fax system and best fax software.

Windows 95/98 users: You have very good built-in fax capability. If you want extra features, check out WinFax by Delrina Corporation.

A standard tabletop fax machine is also useful as a scanner. See "Scanning Without a Scanner" on page 120.

Chapter Twenty-five

Getting the Best Service

This advice alone is worth the cost of this book. When you bring your computer in for servicing, be prepared to answer the following questions:

1. What did the error message say when your computer failed?
2. When did the problem occur—as you turned on the machine? While you were using your modem? At another point? Try to be specific.
3. If the problem occurred more than once, was there a pattern to when it happened?
4. Were you doing anything out of the ordinary when you had the problem?

For additional advice about getting your computer serviced or any clarification, check our Web site, www.geeksquad.com, or call us at 1-800-GEEK-SQUAD (433-5778).

Guidelines When Calling for a Pickup or Dropping the Computer Off for Repair

- Get an RMA (return merchandise authorization) number. This is a confirmation number that protects you in case there is a mistake. It's the company's internal tracking number, and you need it to check the status of your computer as it's being serviced.
- Get a phone number you can call to check the repair status. You may be able to track the repair through the company's Web site, so get the e-mail address, too.
- Whether you bring the computer directly into a store or send it through a shipping company, get a receipt. Unless you ask, it may not be offered.
- If you have had previous problems with your computer, check to see if the warranty contains a lemon clause (see "The Deciding Factor: Service and Support" on page 31).

What to Take to the Service Center

- System disks (floppies or CD).
- Software you're having problems with.

Windows 95/98 users: Bring the small instruction booklet (it has the certificate of authenticity on the cover).

- The computer. *Do not bring the monitor unless you have checked in advance.* The Geeks, like many computer-repair centers, will not deal with monitors.

To leap frog to the head of the line in a superstore, tell the counterperson you are having trouble accessing your erotica. Once you're helped, you can always remember that stuff is on your *other* hard drive.

When Sending Away a Computer Under Warranty

- You need your receipt or the credit-card statement showing that you have a warranty.
- You need the packaging to pack up the computer and take it down to the store. If you have an extended warranty but are missing the packing, the manufacturer may ship it to you before you send the computer. Call the service line to make arrangements. If the computer is not properly packed, it will not arrive in good enough condition to be salvaged.
- When you make your initial contact with any repair person, get the person's name and/or extension number so that you have someone specific to ask for in the event of a problem.
- Send only what you are told to send. When you send in a machine for repairs, the company won't want your cords. Unless specifically discussed, they probably won't want your keyboard or monitor, either. Remove any CDs or floppies in the drive, if you can. Also, don't send your laptop in its case—most likely, you'll never get it back.
- Include a written description of the symptom. When you run into problems, the best thing you can do for yourself is write down what happens, when it happens, and what you did to try to correct the situation. Details, details, details . . .

Very important: If you want to retain the information on your hard drive, state in your letter that when your computer is repaired, the company must back up your material. Otherwise, your hard drive might be replaced, and your files will be lost. If the machine is under warranty, whoever is servicing it is required to do a backup if a request is made.

When the Computer Is Not Under Warranty

Look for a place that offers a flat rate so that you will know up front what it will cost you to get your computer fixed.

When the News Is Bad

If you're told that you need an expensive repair or your hard drive must be reformatted, get a second opinion. Remember, we said to treat it like your dog—you'd get a second opinion for Fido, wouldn't you?

Chapter Twenty-six

Retirement Planning for Your Computer

You've outgrown your machine. Here's what you can do:

Upgrade It

Any computer you buy should serve your needs for three to four years. At that point, you may want a newer machine with more capabilities. Years ago, people upgraded, but that's rarely cost-effective today, especially for anyone who has to pay a technical person to do the installation.

On the other hand, if you want to keep the computer more than four to five years, you may find an upgrade necessary and worthwhile. Even so, there are only three kinds of upgrades that make sense:

- Hard drive: Your computer may be fast enough and do anything you want, but you may be running out of space. Get more. (Cost: about $300.)
- RAM: You may need extra memory to use a particular application or to run several applications at once—for example, to integrate graphics and text. (Cost: about $100.)
- Modem: You may not have a modem at all, or you may need one that is faster, or you may need one that has fax capacity. (Cost: about $100.)

Sell It

If you decide to sell your current system and use the money to purchase a new one—which will probably run about $1,500 and include a new warranty—you can probably count on getting about $400 to $500 for your computer, printer, and monitor (or about

one-third of your original cost). If any one of the three items must be replaced

with a new one, your system won't be a bargain and may be hard to sell. But if you have all the pieces, are charging a reasonable price, and can offer the system with the warranty intact, you should be able to find a buyer.

The warranty, since it's transferable, will add greatly to the resale value. If you can say, "Here's the paperwork; if the machine breaks within the next two to three years, the manufacturer will fix it free of charge," you can have a clear conscience even about selling your old equipment to a friend.

Donate It

If your computer meets the proper specifications, many schools will accept it and give you a credit for the contribution, which you can apply against your income taxes. The amount of the contribution may be higher than the amount you could get for selling the machine.

Keep It

A final alternative: Keep the old machine—without upgrades—for the kids. You won't compete to share time or risk having your data destroyed while they play.

APPENDIX A
BASIC PROCEDURES

Minimum System Startup

Very, very often, people have difficulty starting the machine after they have recently changed something—added a new video card or a sound driver, for example. They may not even make the connection between this addition and the fact that they are having difficulty. So, frequently, when we're making a diagnosis of a problem, we begin by doing a *minimum system startup*.

This requires shutting down the machine, turning off all the drivers/extensions ("drivers" is the Windows word; "extensions" is the Mac word, but they're all referring to any added device or capability and the software that runs it), and restarting so that the computer is performing only basic functions. You can work with the software, but the printer, scanner, and other peripherals won't be in use. If it then works, we can assume that the problem is a driver/extension conflict.

A machine that can't boot up with a minimum system startup has severe problems and needs servicing.

Here's the basic procedure for a minimum system startup:

1. Shut down all external devices. Shut down the computer.
2. Disconnect all external devices except for the keyboard cable, mouse cable, power cable, and video cable.
3. Wait two minutes before restarting a machine, because sometimes the error messages will reappear for a minute or two.
4. Restart.

Mac users: Turn the computer on. As soon as you hear the startup sound, hold down the Shift key and keep holding it until you see the sign that says, "Welcome to Macintosh." Underneath the welcome sign will be the words "extensions off." Let go of the Shift key. When the desktop appears, try to run your program. Since the extensions are off, you can run only your software. Go to step 5.

Windows 3.X users: Get ready to turn the computer on and press the F8 key. Press the key at the instant you see the words "Starting MS-DOS." A

text menu will appear: Choose the option to bypass startup files. Since the extensions are off, you can run only your software, not the printer or other extensions. Go to step 5.

Windows 95/98 users: Have your finger ready on the F5 key and turn the computer on. Press the key at the instant you see the words "Starting Windows." This will get you into Safe Mode, a special diagnostic mode for Windows. When the desktop appears, try to run your program. Since the extensions are off, you can run only your software, not the printer or other extensions. Go to step 5.

5. If you don't see the desktop, bring the machine in for repair.
6. If you do see the desktop, follow the instructions we've given in the appropriate section(s) to change settings, or uninstall or remove whatever changes you just made in the system. The manufacturer of the driver may be able to give you tech support, or see "Resolving Driver/Extension Conflicts–Reinstalling Drivers/Extensions" on page 213.

Reinstalling the Operating System

People worry that if they reinstall the operating-system software, they will lose all the documents they have created. This isn't true, provided you follow the caution messages. The procedure replaces only the operating-system files and doesn't affect your drivers, your application software, or the documents that you have created.

However, before you proceed, try to make a backup of your files if you don't already have one. At minimum, try to back up those files you most urgently need.

If you do have a tape, removable drive, or other backup, you may wonder why you shouldn't dump everything rather than reinstall. It's because once your machine isn't working, most likely, it won't run the backup, either. Also, you don't want to use the stuff in a crashing machine as a backup—what you backed up is probably defective.

Simple Reinstallation

To do the simplest and safest reinstallation, put your operating-system disks in the machine one at a time, following the prompts. In doing this, you overwrite the existing operating-system files. In some cases, this may solve your problem.

 CAUTION: At the beginning or during the process, a message may say that the file you're copying is older than the one on your computer and ask if you want to keep the one that's already on computer. Choose "Yes." But if the reinstallation with the existing drivers doesn't solve the problem, repeat this process, this time choosing "No." If you are prompted to reformat or reinitialize the hard drive, say "No," or you will lose your data.

When you do a simple reinstallation, whatever you've added to the machine—for example, programs to run a fax modem or games, and any documents you have created—will stay there.

If you perform a simple reinstallation and you are still having difficulties, you may have to reinstall the operating system and also remove and reinstall everything else.

Total/Clean Reinstallation

This procedure ensures that you will remove any possible corruption, but it's time-consuming because it requires taking everything off your computer (operating system, programs, drivers, and all documents you've created) and then reinstalling it all. (That's why it's called a clean reinstall—because you're deleting data.)

The trickiest part of this is removing everything properly so that it can all be restored. To be on the safe side, take your computer to the Geek Squad (or, lacking a Geek Squad in your hometown, whatever other repair place you have to settle for). First, do a complete backup. Then, have them remove everything and reinstall the operating system, and probably the drivers as well. (See "Resolving Driver/Extension Conflicts–Reinstalling Drivers/Extensions" on page 213.) Then you can attempt to do the reinstallation of individual applications, such as Microsoft Word or Quicken, on your own. Since installing individual programs is as expensive as installing the operating system (but a lot less tricky), it makes sense to try to save money by doing this on your own.

After the operating systems, drivers, and applications have been installed, you can simply copy the documents you have created from whatever backup method you used—floppies, a removable drive, tape, whatever.

NOTE: "Drivers" is the PC word; "extensions" is the Mac word. They both refer to hardware, including your hard drive, printer, CD-ROM, and so on.

If a minimum system startup removes a particular problem, then the source of the problem is a driver/extension that the computer is trying to load. Here's how to identify which one it is:

Mac users: Restart with the Shift key held down. Drag up to ten extensions out of the Extensions folder and into a temporary folder that you've created on the desktop. Restart. If the problem is gone, one of the extensions you removed is the bad guy. Add the extensions back to the original folder, one at a time, restarting in between each, until your problem returns. The last one you moved is the bad guy. (Note: Never remove the files "Text Encoding Converter" or "Appearance Extension.")

If you make it through the Extensions folder without finding anything, move on to the Control Panel folder. Remove all items into a temporary folder and continue as directed above.

Windows users: Click on Open Settings | Control Panel | System | Device Manager. If a device has a yellow exclamation point, it has been disabled. Select the device and click the Properties button. Listed under Status will be a more-detailed description of the error or conflict.

You will have to reinstall the driver/extension that is creating the problem. Some are easy to reinstall, but others are not—you may want to consult a professional to see which drivers might be simple enough for you to install yourself.

Before you do a reinstall, back up everything. Then, connect the power to the device you are reinstalling, plug the device into the computer, and only then turn it on. Then insert the first installation disk for that device. You should see an "Install" or "Setup" program. Follow the prompts and then do a test of the device.

Continue with the same procedure for the remaining devices. If any one isn't working properly, refer to the section of this book where it is discussed in detail (for example, printers, CD-ROMs, whatever).

APPENDIX B
YEAR 2000 (Y2K) PROBLEMS

Y2K problems may affect hardware, operating systems, or software. Here's how to anticipate them. (Remember: If all three elements are not compliant, no single one of them will work.)

Hardware

Mac users: Problems unlikely. Check the Apple Web site at www.apple.com/macos/info/2000.html.

Windows users: To test whether your hardware is vulnerable (especially if your machine was bought in 1997 or earlier), check the BIOS (basic input/output system) that accesses the date and time in the brain of the machine. First close your applications and back up everything. Then proceed as follows:

Windows 95/98 users: Go to Control Panel | Date/Time. Change the date to December 31, 1999, and the time to 11:58:00 P.M., then click OK. Go to step 2.

Windows 3/X users: Go to the MS-DOS prompt, type "Time" and hit Enter, type "Date" and hit Enter, type "12-31-99" and hit Enter, and type "Exit" and hit Enter. Go to step 2.

2. Turn off your computer, wait several minutes, then reboot. Check to see if the date has properly rolled over to January 1, 2000.
3. Retest by moving the date to January 2 and reboot.
4. If you see the wrong date, have a service person modify or replace your BIOS.

NOTE: Free PC hardware testing tools can also be downloaded from Test 2000 (www.righttime.com) and Ymark2000 (www.nstl.com).

Operating System

Mac users: No problems expected.

Windows 98 users: No problems expected.

Windows 95 and Windows 3.5 users: Go to Control Panel | Regional Settings. Reset Short-Date Format from mm-dd-yy to mm-dd-yyyy. This should tell your programs to run on a four-digit-year mode.

Software

Check with each manufacturer for potential problems.

Don't use two-digit years to store information on spreadsheets or database programs.

Don't download date-sensitive material from the Internet.

APPENDIX C
DEFINITIONS

Applications: The various programs that allow your computer to do different kinds of jobs. There may be a word-processing application that lets you type, a graphics application that lets you draw, and so on for other capabilities. Applications are sometimes referred to as "software" or "programs."

Boot up: Means "start," or "turn the power on" by flipping the switch. The machine is not considered to be booted up until it's ready for use: the screen is lit and the icons for the hard drive and other elements appear on the screen.

CPU (Central Processing Unit): The brain of the computer. A Pentium chip is a CPU. It is also used, loosely, to refer to the unit containing the disk drives.

Driver/Extension: The IBM people call them "drivers," and the Mac people call them "extensions." They're referring to hardware such as a printer, modem, scanner, digital camera that comes on floppy disk or CD-ROM, removable disk drive, mouse, modem, sound card, and so on—though technically, the "driver" is not really the hardware itself, but the software that allows your computer to control it.

Hard drive: A little metal box inside your computer where everything is permanently stored—the operating system, the applications (which are the programs that allow you to do your word processing or accounting, and play your games), and the documents (which are whatever you create on the machine). It contains a disk that spins like a record player and a magnetic needle that reads the information. *See also* RAM.

Modem: Device that connects computer to a phone line so that you can get onto the Internet. Most modems can also send and receive faxes.

Motherboard (logic board): The device that all other devices plug into, and that allows them all to work together.

OCR (optical character recognition): In scanning, a capability that allows the machine to read text and convert it into editable form.

Operating system: Together with the hard drive, the main operating system makes the computer run. There are also operating systems that control each of the drivers. All operating systems are considered software and come on one or more floppy disks or on a CD. It is absolutely critical that you have these stored safely.

Power up: *See* Boot up.

Programs: *See* Applications; Software.

RAM (random-access memory): When you turn on the computer and select a particular document, the hard drive moves whatever material you need onto little chips (RAM) that are at the end of plastic sticks a couple of inches long. When you turn the computer off, the chips empty, and whatever material they were holding is gone. That is why we say that RAM is for temporary storage. When you start up your computer, system software (including most drivers/extensions and control panels) loads automatically into RAM, and applications load into RAM when you click on them.

Beginning computer users have trouble distinguishing between the hard drive and the RAM. Think of the hard drive as a file cabinet, where everything is permanently stored, and the RAM is a desktop: You pull files out of the cabinet and put them temporarily on the desktop. If you have a great many current files, you need a larger desktop so that you can create and edit and process your documents, and adding RAM is like adding desktop space. *See also* Hard drive.

Resolution: The amount of pixels or information that can be displayed on the monitor screen at one time.

Scanner: If you want to bring a magazine or newspaper article or photograph into the computer, you use a scanner. If you don't have a scanner but want to get the same effect, see "Scanning Without a Scanner" on page 120.

SCSI (small computer systems interface, or "scuzzy") devices: Related to a Mac. These include printers, scanners, external hard drives, CD-ROM drives, and others. As many as six SCSI devices can be connected in an unbroken chain that is plugged into the large SCSI port on the back of the Mac. Each device must

have a unique number between 0 and 7 (selected on the back of the device by wheel or button). The internal hard drive, for example, has number 0 and CD-ROM drives usually are assigned number 3.

Software: Anything that isn't hardware. Thus software includes the operating system, the applications (or programs), and the documents you create. Sometimes software is used to refer only to applications (or programs).

Sound card: A device that enables your Windows-based computer to handle sound and that works in conjunction with speakers. We recommend Sound-Blaster, which has become the de facto industry standard.

APPENDIX D
RESOURCES

If you have trouble with any of the information in this book or if you have a computer problem you cannot solve, you can reach the Geek Squad twenty-four hours a day at 1-800-GEEK-SQUAD (433-5778). You can also visit us at our Web site at www.geeksquad.com.

PC SOFTWARE/HARDWARE

APS Tech*	800-395-5871	www.apstech.com
CDW	800-835-4239	www.cdw.com
DataComm Warehouse	800-397-8508	www.warehouse.com
Dell	800-WWW-DELL	www.dell.com
Gateway 2000	800-846-4208	www.gateway.com
Global Computer	800-8GLOBAL	www.globalcomputer.com
Micro Warehouse	800-397-8508	www.warehouse.com
Micron	888-224-4247	www.micron.com
PC Mall	800-863-3282	www.pcmall.com
PC Warehouse	800-397-8508	www.warehouse.com
PC Zone	800-408-9663	www.pczone.com

MAC SOFTWARE/HARDWARE

APS Tech*	800-395-5871	www.apstech.com
CDW	800-835-4239	www.cdw.com
Club Mac	800-258-2622	www.clubmac.com
DataComm Warehouse	800-397-8508	www.warehouse.com
Inmac	800-547-5444	www.inmac.com
Mac Mall	800-328-2790	www.macmall.com
Mac Warehouse	800-397-8508	www.warehouse.com
Mac Zone	888-211-5032	www.maczone.com

*Hardware only

PC PARTS

PC Service Source	800-727-2787	www.pcss.com (new and used)
Spartan Technologies	888-393-0340	www.spartantech.com (new)

MAC PARTS/REPAIR

DT&T Mac Services	800-622-7967	www.dtservice.com (used)
Shreve Systems	800-227-3971	www.shrevesystems.com (new and used)

LCD REPAIR (PC)

Matrix International	800-622-2549	www.matrixintl.com

MONITOR SYNCH ADAPTORS (MAC/PC)

Griffin Technology	615-255-0990	www.griffintechnology.com

REMOTE BACKUP SERVICES

Connected Online	888-922-2587	www.connected.com
Mailsafe	888-333-6344	www.ms-offsite.com
Offsite Backup Data Management Services	718-789-3578	www.odms.com

PRICE COMPARISONS (check these sites to compare prices)

www.pricewatch.com

www.buycomp.com

www.netbuyer.com

www.computershopper.com

INDEX